Stories of the Highland Clearances

BLOODSHED AND BETRAYAL IN THE GLENS

Alexander Mackenzie

Lang**Syne**

PUBLISHING

WRITING *to* REMEMBER

WRITING *to* REMEMBER

Strathclyde Business Centre
120 Carstairs Street, Glasgow G40 4JD
Tel: 0141 554 9944 Fax: 0141 554 9955
E-mail: scottishmemories@aol.com
www.scottish-memories.co.uk

Printed by JSB Print, Glasgow
© Lang Syne Publishers Ltd 2003
ISBN 0-946264-68-6

Stories of the Highland Clearances

Introduction

In these pages the full horrifying story of the Highland Clearances unfolds.

Man's inhumanity to man was brought sharply into focus in those grim days of the early nineteenth century when entire communities were swept away so that the land could be sold off to southern sheep farmers.

These were times of betrayal and bravery and of cruelty and deception.

There was betrayal of the people by the clan chiefs who, after the fiasco of the '45, had no need for heroic men to fight their wars. Power now lay in money realised from the sale of land — not in land won and kept in battle by loyal men who gave their blood for the soil.

Even the clergy betrayed their flocks who were largely illiterate but deeply religious and God fearing folk. Highlanders saw the minister as the stern oracle of the truth but, sadly, he was often the puppet of the estate whose power he feared and whose support he received. The theme from pulpit to pew was that troubles were merely part of the punishment inflicted by Providence in the course of man working out his redemption.

Bravery was the hallmark of the folk forced to leave these shores for the Americas and Australia. Conditions on the emigrant ships were horrific with travellers packed together like sardines regardless of comfort and the decencies of life and with insufficient food. Many died from disease and famine. Those who made it encountered sub zero or very high temperatures to which they couldn't adjust. In America many were abandoned and massacred by Red Indians. Others had to tramp for weeks through trackless forests to Upper Canada where there were settlements of fellow Scots who could provide food and shelter.

Through time, though, hundreds of these emigrants prospered and lived to enjoy a good life in the New World. Back home things, ironically, turned full cycle and some of their worst oppressors fell on hard times.

The cruelty displayed by the evicting mobs is vividly described from eye-witness accounts taken at the time. Even the old sick and infirm were tossed out into the heather and their homes pulled down around their ears. Many tenants died from alarm, fatigue and cold. Those who lived attempted to build makeshift homes from old bits of wood and trees but always the laird's men would come and demolish even these humble efforts. One family tried to find shelter living in a graveyard but even that was not permitted.

There was deception of the people at home and abroad by the estate owners and their factors. Clearances were necessary to make better use of the land as sheep would contribute more to the well being of the country generally than crofters and cows it was argued. Displaced families could make a good living on the coast and from the sea. Nobody was forced to emigrate. But in reality hundreds ended up living on rocky land along the water's edge and their only food was cockles picked from the shore supplemented by mixing cattle blood with oatmeal which was cut into slices and fried. And, all too often, entire families were taken from their homes and put on ships for distant lands on the other side of the world.

Most of the material was written by Alexander Mackenzie and first published in 1883. The selection of stories and experiences featured here is taken from the 1914 edition produced by E. Mackay of Stirling.

An introduction to this later edition refers to Mr Mackenzie as a Highlander "who commanded in a great measure the esteem of fellow Highlanders and collected for the first time the sane and authenticated accounts of the experiences of the people in the great agrarian crisis of their history.

"The Highlander loves his past and the story of the great wrongs of the days of the clearances is still deeply embedded in his mind.

"Nowhere have blacker or more foul deeds been committed in the name of property than in the Highlands of Scotland in those days".

The great Sir Walter Scott, who made frequent attacks on the activities of the big landowners, wrote: "The Highlands have been drained of a whole mass of inhabitants, dispossessed by an unrelenting avarice, which will one day be found to have been as short sighted as it is unjust and selfish".

All chapters are by Alexander Mackenzie unless otherwise stated. Copy has been shortened or rewritten in certain passages for ease of reading.

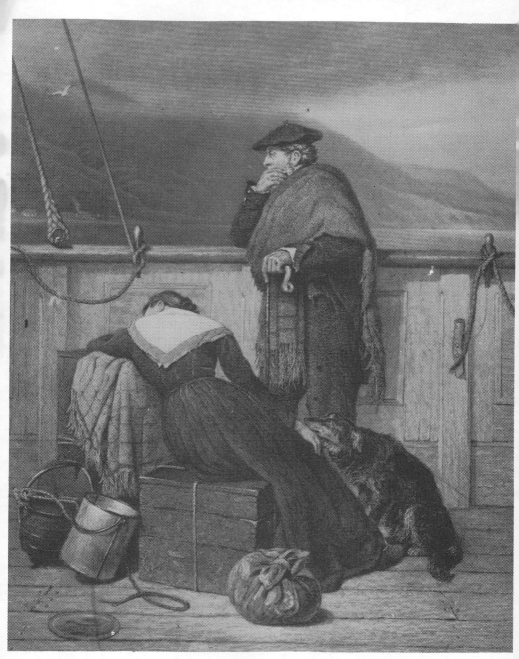

"Lochaber No More" — from an engraving by Charles Couseu
after a painting by J Watson Nicol.
(Courtesy BBC Hulton Picture Library).

A REAL "SCOTTISH GRIEVANCE."

DUNCAN.—"Oh! but my mother is frail, and can't be sent out of the country in that ship; will you not let Flora and her———"
FACTOR.—[sternly] "No, no lad—more on with the old woman; she will not be here in the way of his Lordship's sheep and deer."

Courtesy: Mitchell Library, Glasgow

"The Injustice so palpable, the inhumanity so great".
Two views from Donald Ross's Real Scottish Grievances. The upper one refers to Lord Macdonald's evictions at Boreraig on Skye. (Courtesy: Mitchell Library, Glasgow).

'The Last of the Clan — 1851' by J C Brown

Although not a scene depicted as a clearance this Highland Bride's departure gives a vivid picture of folk in those times. (Picture courtesy of Sotheby's).

LIVINGSTONE'S

CALEDONIAN CRITIC.

"LET YOUR MASTERS COME AND ATTACK US, WE ARE READY TO MEET THEM."—
SIR WILLIAM WALLACE.

No. 1.] FEBRUARY, 1852. [PRICE 2D.

PROSPECTUS

IN presenting these pages to the public, we have only to intimate—

1st. That a shameful and criminal neglect of truthfully representing the national character prevailed to a lamentable extent, for the last century at least. That the origin of that evil had its rise among a class of designing men, who transmitted the said rancorous animosity to their posterity to the present day. That from the same source emanated that sweeping flood of oppression, defamation, vice, ignorance, and undisguised Heathenism, which now prevail to so alarming an extent, that there is little hope of National Reform. Nevertheless, it is a Christian duty, binding upon every Scot, who have the least spark of Christian principle—binding upon every man in this kingdom, who can claim Caledonia for their mother, to unite, and come boldly out to develope her national character, in all its bearings—to develope her vast literary resources, buried by her enemies, many of which are among her own ungrateful sons, to develope the fact, that she is indeed the first of the European nations who set bounds to the highest political power that ever existed; and that she is the last of the Euro-

B

Starving Sutherland folk sail to new life in America

To give a proper account of the Sutherland Clearances would take a bulky volume. Indeed, a large tome of 354 pages has been written and published in their defence by him who was mainly responsible for them, called "An Account of the Sutherland Improvements", by James Loch, at that time Commissioner for the Marchioness of Stafford and heiress of Sutherland.

This was the first account I ever read of these so-called improvements; and it was quite enough to convince me, and it will be sufficient to convince anyone who knows anything of the country, that the improvement of the people, by driving them in the most merciless and cruel manner from the homes of their fathers, was carried out on a huge scale and in the most inconsiderate and heartless manner by those in charge of the Sutherland estates.

But when one reads the other side, Macleod's "Gloomy Memories", General Stewart of Garth's "Sketches of the Highlanders", and other contemporary publications, one wonders that such iniquities could ever have been permitted in Britain, which has done so much for the oppressed in every part of the world, while her own brave sons have been persecuted, oppressed, and banished without compensation by greedy proprietors, who owed their position and their lands to the ancestors of the very men they were now treating so cruelly.

The motives of the landlords, generally led by southern factors worse than themselves, were, in most cases, pure self-interest, and they pursued their policy of extermination with recklessness and remorselessness.

Generally, law and justice, religion and humanity, were either totally disregarded, or, what was worse, in many cases converted into and applied as instruments of oppression.

Every conceivable means, short of the musket and the sword, were used to drive the natives from the land they loved, and to force them to exchange their crofts and homes —

brought originally into cultivation and built by themselves, or by their forefathers — for wretched patches among the barren rocks on the sea shore, and to depend, after losing their cattle and their sheep, and after having their houses burnt about their ears or razed to the ground, on the uncertain produce of the sea for subsistence.

What was true generally of the Highlands, was in the county of Sutherland carried to the greatest extreme.

That unfortunate county, according to an eye-witness, was made another Moscow.

The inhabitants were literally burnt out, and every contrivance and cruelty was adopted for extirpating the race.

Many lives were sacrificed by famine and other hardships and privations; hundreds, stripped of their all, emigrated to the Canadas and other parts of America; great numbers, especially of the young and athletic, sought employment in the Lowlands and in England.

The aged and infirm, the widows and orphans, with those of their families who could not think of leaving them alone in their helplessness, were induced to accept the wretched allotments offered them on the wild moors and barren rocks.

The mild nature and religious training of the Highlanders prevented a resort to the resistance and revenge which has repeatedly set bounds to the rapacity of landlords in Ireland.

Their ignorance of the English language, and the want of natural leaders, made it impossible for them to make their grievances known to the outside world.

They were, therefore, maltreated with impunity. The ministers generally sided with the oppressing lairds, who had the Church patronage at their disposal for themselves and for their sons.

The professed ministers of religion sanctioned the iniquity, "the foulest deeds were glossed over, and all the evil which could not be attributed to the natives themselves, such as severe seasons, famines, and consequent disease, was by these pious gentlemen ascribed to Providence, as a punishment for sin".

South countrymen were introduced and the land given to them for sheep farms over the heads of the native tenantry. These strangers were made justices of the peace and armed with all sorts of authority in the county, and thus enabled to act in the most harsh and tyrannical fashion.

The seventeen parish ministers, with the single exception of the Rev Mr Sage, took the side of the powers that were, exhorting the people to submit and to stifle their cries of distress.

Most of these ministers have since rendered their account, and let us hope they have been forgiven for such cruel and blasphemous conduct.

The Sutherland clearances were commenced in a comparatively mild way in 1807, by the ejection of ninety families from Farr and Lairg.

These were provided for some fifteen or seventeen miles distant with smaller lots, to which they were permitted to remove their cattle and plenishing, leaving their crops unprotected, however, in the ground from which they were evicted.

They had to pull down their old houses, remove the timber, and build new ones, during which period they had in many cases to sleep in the open.

In the autumn they carried away, with great difficulty, what remained of their crops, but the fatigue incurred cost a few of them their lives, while others contracted diseases which stuck to them during the remainder of their lives, and shortened their days.

In 1809 several hundred were evicted from the parishes of Dornoch, Rogart, Loth, Clyne, and Golspie, under circumstances of much greater severity.

Several were driven by various means to leave the country altogether, and to those who could not be induced to do so, patches of moor and bog were offered on Dornoch Moor and Brora Links — quite unfit for cultivation.

This process was carried on annually until, in 1811, the land from which the people were ejected was divided into large farms, and advertised as huge sheep runs.

The country was overrun with strangers who came to look at these extensive tracts. Some of these gentlemen got up a cry that they were afraid of their lives among the evicted tenantry.

A trumped-up story was manufactured that one of the interlopers was pursued by some of the natives from Kildonan, and put in bodily fear.

The military were sent for from Fort George. The 21st Regiment was marched to Dunrobin Castle, with artillery and cartloads of ammunition.

A great farce was performed; the people were sent for by the factors to the Castle at a certain hour.

They came peaceably, but the farce must be gone through, the Riot Act was read; a few sheepish, innocent Highlanders were made prisoners, but nothing could be laid to their charge, and they were almost immmediately set at liberty, while the soldiers were ordered back to Fort George.

The demonstration, however, had the desired effect in cowing and frightening the people into the most absolute submission. They became dismayed and broken hearted, and quietly submitted to their fate.

The clergy all this time were assiduous in preaching that all the misfortunes of the people were "fore-ordained of God, and denouncing the vengeance of Heaven and eternal damnation on all those who would presume to make the slightest resistance".

At the May term of 1812 large districts of these parishes were cleared in the most peaceable manner, the poor creatures foolishly believing the false teaching of their selfish and dishonest spiritual guides.

The Earl of Selkirk, who went personally to the district, allured many of the evicted people to emigrate to his estates on the Red River in British North America. A whole ship-cargo of them went.

After a long and otherwise disastrous passage they found themselves deceived and deserted by the Earl, left to their unhappy fate in an inclement wilderness, without any protection from the hordes of Red Indian savages by whom the district was infested, and who plundered them of their all on their arrival and finally massacred them. Only a small remnant managed to escape, and travelled, through immense difficulties, across trackless forests to Upper Canada.

The notorious Mr Sellar was at this time sub-factor, and in the spring of 1814 he took a large portion of the parishes of Farr and Kildonan into his own hands.

In the month of March the old tenantry received notices to quit at the ensuing May term, and a few days after the summonses were served the greater portion of the heath pasture was, by his orders, set on fire.

By this cruel proceeding the cattle belonging to the old tenantry were left without food during the spring, and it was impossible to dispose of them at a fair price, the price having fallen after the war; for Napoleon was now a prisoner in Elba, and the demand for cattle fell and prices were very much reduced.

To make matters worse, fodder was unusually scarce this spring, and the poor people's cattle depended for subsistence solely on the spring grass which sprouts out among the heather, but which this year had been burnt by the factor who would himself reap the benefit when he came into possession later on.

In May the work of ejectment was again commenced, accompanied by cruelties hitherto unknown even in the Highlands.

Atrocities were perpetrated which I cannot trust myself to describe in my own words. I shall give what is much more valuable — a description by an eye-witness in his own language.

He says:- In former removals the tenants had been allowed to carry away the timber of their old dwellings to erect houses on their new allotments, but now a more summary mode was adopted by setting fire to them.

The able-bodied men were by this time away after their cattle or otherwise engaged at a distance, so that the immediate sufferers by the general house-burning that now commenced were the aged and infirm, the women and children.

As the lands were now in the hands of the factor himself, and were to be occupied as sheep farms, and as the people made no resistance, they expected, at least, some indulgence in the way of permission to occupy their houses and other buildings until they could gradually remove, and meanwhile look after their growing crops.

Their consternation was therefore greater, when immediately after the May term-day, a commencement was made to pull down and set fire to the houses over their heads.

The old people, women and others, then began to preserve the timber which was their own; but the devastators proceeded with the greatest celerity, demolishing all before them, and when they had overthrown all the houses in a large tract of country they set fire to the wreck.

Timber, furniture, and every other article that could not be instantly removed was consumed by fire or otherwise utterly destroyed.

At these scenes Mr Sellar was present, and apparently, as sworn by several witnesses at his subsequent trial, ordering and directing the whole.

Many deaths ensued from alarm, from fatigue, and cold.

Some old men took to the woods and to the rocks, wandering about in a state approaching to, or of absolute, insanity; and several of them in this situation lived only a few days.

Pregnant women were taken in premature labour, and several children did not long survive their sufferings.

"To these scenes", says Donald Macleod, author of Gloomy Memories, "I was an eye-witness, and am ready to substantiate the truth of my statements, not only by my own testimony, but by that of many others who were present at the time.

In such a scene of general devastation, it is almost useless to particularise the cases of individuals; the suffering was great and universal.

I shall, however, notice a very few of the extreme cases of which I was myself an eye-witness. John Mackay's wife, Ravigill, in attempting to pull down her house, in the absence of her husband, to preserve the timber, fell through the roof.

She was in consequence taken in premature labour, and in that state was exposed to the open air and to the view of all the bystanders.

Donald Munro, Garvott, lying in a fever, was turned out of his house and exposed to the elements.

Donald Macbeath, an infirm and bed-ridden old man, had the house unroofed over him, and was in that state exposed to the wind and rain until death put a period to his sufferings.

I was present at the pulling down and burning of the house of William Chisholm, Badinloskin, in which was lying his wife's mother, an old bed-ridden woman of nearly 100 years of age, none of the family being present.

I informed the persons about to set fire to the house of this circumstance, and prevailed on them to wait until Mr Sellar came. On his arrival I told him of the poor old woman being in a condition unfit for removal, when he replied, 'Damn her, the old witch, she has lived too long — let her burn'.

Fire was immediately set to the house, and the blankets in which she was carried out were in flames before she could be got out.

She was placed in a little shed, and it was with great difficulty they were prevented fom firing it also.

The old woman's daughter arrived while the house was on fire, and assisted the neighbours in removing her mother out of the flames and smoke, presenting a picture of horror which I shall never forget, but cannot attempt to describe. Within five days she was a corpse".

In 1816 Sellar was charged at Inverness, before the Court of Justiciary, with culpable homicide and fire-raising in connection with these proceedings, but acquitted of the grave charges made against him.

Almost immediately after, however, he ceased to be factor on the Sutherland estates, and Mr Loch came into power.

Evictions were carried out from 1814 down to 1819 and 1820, pretty much of the same character as those already described, but the removal of Mr Young, the chief factor, and Mr Sellar from power was hailed with delight by the whole remaining population.

The night I counted 250 blazing houses

The people, however, soon discovered that the new factors were not much better. Several leases which were current would not expire until 1819 and 1820, so that the evictions were necessarily only partial from 1814 down to that period.

The people were reduced to such a state of poverty that even Mr Loch himself, in his "Sutherland Improvements", page 76, admits that — "Their wretchedness was so great that, after pawning everything they possessed to the fishermen on the coast, such as had no cattle were reduced to come down from the hills in hundreds for the purpose of gathering cockles on the shore.

Those who lived in the more remote situations of the country were obliged to subsist upon broth made of nettles, thickened with a little oatmeal.

Those who had cattle had recourse to the still more wretched expedient of bleeding them, and mixing the blood with oatmeal, which they afterwards cut into slices and fried.

Those who had a little money came down and slept all night upon the beach, in order to watch the boats returning from the fishing, that they might be in time to obtain a part of what had been caught".

He, however, omitted to mention the share he and his predecessors had taken in reducing the people to such misery, and the fact that at this very time he had constables stationed at the Little Ferry to prevent the starved tenantry from collecting shellfish in the only place where they could find them.

He prevailed upon the people to sign documents consenting to move at the next Whitsunday term, promising at the same time to make good provision for them elsewhere.

In about a month after, the work of demolition and devastation again commenced, and parts of the parishes of Golspie, Rogart, Farr, and the whole of Kildonan were in a blaze.

Strong parties with faggots and other combustible material were set to work; three hundred houses were given ruthlessly to the flames, and their occupants pushed out into the open air without food or shelter.

Macleod, who was present, describes the horrible scene as follows:-

"The consternation and confusion were extreme; little or no time was given for the removal of persons or property; the people striving to remove the sick and the helpless before the fire should reach them; next, struggling to save the most valuable of their effects.

The cries of the women and children, the roaring of the affrighted cattle, hunted at the same time by the yelling dogs of the shepherds amid the smoke and fire, altogether presented a scene that completely baffles description.

A dense cloud of smoke enveloped the whole country by day, and even extended far out to sea; at night an awfully grand but terrific scene presented itself - all the houses in an extensive district in flames at once.

I myself ascended a height about eleven o'clock in the evening, and counted two hundred and fifty blazing houses, many of the owners of which were my relations, and all of whom I personally knew, but whose present condition — whether in or out of the flames — I could not tell.

The conflagration lasted six days, till the whole of the dwellings were reduced to ashes or smoking ruins".

The whole of the inhabitants of Kildonan, numbering nearly 2000 souls, except three families, were utterly rooted and burnt out, and the whole parish converted into a soltary wilderness.

The suffering was intense. Some lost their reason. Over a hundred souls took passage to Caithness in a small sloop, the master humanely agreeing to take them in the hold, from which he had just unloaded a cargo of quicklime.

A head storm came on, and they were nine days at sea in the most miserable condition — men, women, and helpless children huddled up together, with barely any provisions. Several died.

The beautiful Strathnaver, containing a population equal to Kildonan, had been cleared in the same heartless manner.

In 1828, Donald Macleod, after a considerable absence, returned to his native Kildonan, where he attended service in the parish church, with a congregation consisting of eight shepherds and their dogs — numbering between twenty and thirty — the minister, and three members of his family.

Macleod came in too late for the first psalm, but at the conclusion of the service the fine old tune Bangor was given out, "when the four-footed hearers became excited, got up on the seats, and raised a most infernal chorus of howling.

Their masters attacked them with their crooks, which only made matters worse; the yelping and howling continued to the end of the service".

And Donald Macleod retired to contemplate the painful and shameful scene, and contrast it with what he had previously experienced as a member, for many years, of the large and devout congregation that worshipped formerly in the parish church of his native valley.

The Parish Church of Farr was no longer in existence; the fine population of Strathnaver was rooted and burnt out during the general conflagration, and presented a similar aspect to his own native parish.

The church, no longer found necessary, was razed to the ground, and its timbers conveyed to construct one of the Sutherland "improvements" — the Inn at Altnaharra, while the minister's house was converted into a dwelling for a fox-hunter.

Don't bother paying any rent — we want your land for sheep

By the Rev Donald Sage

I remained for about a year in the capacity of tutor in the family of Mr Robert MacKid, Sheriff-Substitute of Sutherland, who lived at Kirkton, in the parish of Golspie. I shall briefly sum up what I remember of this period.

It was a very short time previous to my residence in Mr MacKid's family that the first "Sutherland Clearance" took place. This consisted in the ejection from their minutely-divided farms of several hundreds of the Sutherland aborigines, who had from time immemorial been in possession of their mountain tenements.

This sweeping desolation extended over many parishes, but it fell most heavily on the parish of Kildonan. It was the device of one William Young, a successful corn-dealer and land-improver.

He rose from indigence, but was naturally a man of taste, of an ingenious turn of mind, and a shrewd calculator.

After realising some hundreds of pounds by corn-dealing, he purchased a small and valueless property in Morayshire called Inverugie.

It lay upon the sea-shore, and, like many properties of more ancient date, it had been completely covered with sea-sand which had drifted upon its surface.

For this small and worthless spot he paid a correspondingly small price — about £700 — but, tasking his native and vigorous genius for improvement, he set himself at once to better his bargain.

Making use of a plough of peculiar construction, he turned the sand down and the rich old soil up, and thus made it one of the most productive properties in the county.

This, with other necessary improvements, however, involved him in debt; but, just as it became a question with him how to pay it, his praise in the north as a scientific improver of land reached the ears of the wealthy Stafford family, who wanted to improve their Highland estate.

As Young had been so successful on the estate of Inverugie they thought he could be equally so on the Sutherland estate.

Young introduuced the depopulating system into Sutherland. This system, during his tenure of office as commissioner on the Sutherland property, was just at its commencement. It was first brought to bear on the parish of Kildonan.

The whole north and south sides of the Strath, from Kildonan to Caen on the left bank of the river, and from Dalcharn to Marrel on the right bank, were, at one fell sweep, cleared of their inhabitants.

The measures for their ejectment had been taken with such promptness, and were so suddenly and brutally carried out, as to excite a tumult among the people.

Young had as his associate in the factorship a man of the name of Sellar, who acted in the subordinate capacity of legal agent and accountant on the estate, and who, by his unprincipled recklessness in conducting the process of ejectment, added fuel to the flame.

It was said that the people rose almost *en masse*. The

constables and officials were resisited and their lives threatened.

Eventually the Sheriff-Depute of the county called in the military to quell the riot.

A detachment of soldiers was sent from Fort-George, a powder magazine was erected at Dornoch, and every preparation made for the commencement of a civil war.

But the chief magistrate of the county, shrewdly suspecting the origin of these reports, ordered back the military, came himself alone among the people, and instituted a cool and impartial enquiry into their proceedings.

The result was that the formidable riot, which was reported to have for its objects the murder of Young and Sellar, the expulsion of the store-farmers, and the burning of Dunrobin Castle, amounted after all only to this, that a certain number of the people had congregated in different places and had given vent to their outraged feelings and sense of oppression in rash and unguarded terms.

It could not be proved that a single act of violence was committed. Sellar laboured hard to involve my father and mother in the criminality of these proceedings, but he utterly failed.

The peasantry, as fine as any in the world, were treated by the owners of the soil as "good for nothing but to be cast out and trodden under feet of men", while the tract of country thus depopulated was divided into two large sheep farms.

The reckless lordly proprietors had resolved upon the expulsion of their long-standing tenantry from their widely-extended estates, and the Sutherland Clearance of 1819 was not only the climax of their system of oppression for many years before, but the extinction of the last remnant of the ancient Highland peasantry in the north.

As violent tempests send out before them many a deep and sullen roar, so did the advancing storm give notice of its approach by various single acts of oppression.

I can yet recall to memory the deep and thrilling sensation which I experienced, when the tidings of the meditated removal of my poor flock first reached me from headquarters. It might be about the beginning of October, 1818.

A tenant from the middle of the Strath had been to Rhives, the residence of Mr Young, the commissioner, paying his rent. He was informed, and authorised to tell his neighbours, that the rent for the half-year, ending in May, 1819, would not be demanded, as it was intended to lay the districts of Strathnaver and Upper Kildonan under sheep.

This intelligence when first announced was indignantly discredited by the people. Notwithstanding their knowledge of former clearances they clung to the hope that the "Banmhorair Chataibh" (the Duchess of Sutherland) would not give her consent to the warning as issued by her subordinates, and thus deprive herself of her people. But the course of a few weeks soon proved them wrong.

Summonses of ejectment were issued and despatched all over the district. These must have amounted to upwards of a thousand, as the population of the Mission alone was 1600 souls, and many more than those of the Mission were ejected.

The summonses were distributed with the utmost preciseness. They were handed in at every house and hovel alike.

The enormous amount of citations might be accounted for by the fact that Mr Peter Sellar had a threefold personal interest in the whole matter. He was, in the first place, factor on the Sutherland estate at the time; then, he was law agent for the proprietors; and, lastly, the lessee or tacksman of more than a third of the county to be cleared of its inhabitants.

It may easily be conceived how such a three-plied cord of worldly interest would bind him over to greater rigour, and even atrocity, in executing the orders of his superiors on the wretched people among whom he was let loose.

But the effects produced by these decided measures I now distinctly remember. Having myself, in common with the rest of my people, received one of these notices, I resolved that, at the ensuing term of Martinmas, I would remove from Achness, and go once more permanently to reside under my father's roof, although I would at the same time continue the punctual discharge of my pastoral duties among the people till they also should be removed.

I could not but regard the summoning of the minister as tantamount to the putting down of the ministration of the Word and ordinances of religion in that part of the country. And, indeed, it is a fact, that, although this desolate district is still occupied by shepherds, no provision has, since that time, been made for their spiritual wants.

I left Achness, therefore, about the middle of November, 1818, sold my cow at the Ardgay market, and got my furniture conveyed to Kildonan by my father's horses and my own.

The people received the legal warning to leave for ever the homes of their fathers with a sort of stupor — that apparent indifference which is often the external aspect of intense feeling.

As they began, however, to awaken from the stunning effects of this first intimation, their feelings found vent, and I was much struck with the different ways in which they expressed their sentiments.

The truly pious acknowledged the mighty hand of God in the matter. In their prayers and religious conferences not a solitary expression could be heard indicative of anger or vindictiveness, but in the sight of God they humbled themselves, and received the chastisement at His hand.

Those, however, who were strangers to the Gospel breathed deep and muttered curses on the heads of the persons who subjected them to such treatment.

The more reckless portion of them fully realised the character of the impenitent in all ages, and indulged in the most culpable excesses, even while this divine punishment was still suspended over them.

These last, however, were very few in number — not more than a dozen.

To my poor and defenceless flock the dark hour of trial came at last in right earnest. It was in the month of April, and about the middle of it, that they were all — man, woman, and child — from the heights of Farr to the mouth of the Naver, on one day, to quit their tenements and go — many of them knew not whither.

For a few, some miserable patches of ground along the shores were doled out as lots, without aught in the shape of the poorest hut to shelter them.

Upon those lots it was intended that they should build houses at their own expense, and cultivate the ground, at the same time occupying themselves as fishermen, although the great majority of them had never set foot on a boat in their lives. Thither, therefore, they were driven, at a week's warning.

As for the rest most of them did not know where to go, unless their neighbours on the shore provided them with a temporary shelter; for, on the day of their removal, they would not be allowed to remain, even on the bleakest moor, and in the open air, for a distance of twenty miles around.

Widow's heartache

The middle of the week brought on the day of the Strathnaver Clearance (1819). It was a Tuesday.

At an early hour of that day Mr Sellar, accompanied by the Fiscal, and escorted by a strong body of constables, sheriff-officers and others, commenced work at Grummore, the first inhabited township to the west of the Achness district.

Their plan of operations was to clear the cottages of their inmates, giving them about half-an-hour to pack up and carry off their furniture, and then set the cottages on fire.

They ruthlessly adhered to this plan without the sightest regard to any obstacle that might arise.

At Grumbeg lived a soldier's widow, Henny Munro.

She was a joyous, cheery old creature; so inoffensive, moreover, and so contented, and brimful of good-will that all who got acquainted with her could only desire to do her a good turn.

Surely the factor and his followers did not personally know old Henny, or they could not have treated her as they did.

After the cottages at Grummore were emptied of their inmates, and roofs and rafters had been lighted up into one red blaze, Mr Sellar and his iron-hearted attendants approached the residence of the soldier's widow.

Henny stood up to plead for her furniture — the coarsest and most valueless that well could be, but still her earthly all.

She first asked that, as her neighbours were so occupied with their own furniture, hers might be allowed to remain till they should be free to remove it for her.

This request was curtly refused. She then asked if a shepherd who was present could remove the furniture to his own residence on the opposite shore of the loch, to remain there till she could carry it away.

This also was refused, and she was told, with an oath, that if she did not take her trumpery off within half-an-hour it would be burned.

The poor widow had only to task the remains of her bodily strength, and address herself to the work of dragging her chests, beds, presses, and stools out at the door, and placing them at the gable of her cottage.

No sooner was her task accomplished than the torch was applied, the widow's hut, built of very combustible material, speedily ignited, and there rose up rapidly, first a dense cloud of smoke, and soon thereafter a bright red flame.

The wind unfortunately blew in the direction of the furniture, and the flame, lighting upon it, speedily reduced it to ashes.

In their progress down the Strath, Ceann-na-coille was the next township reached by the fire-raising evictors.

An aged widow lived there, who, by infirmity, had been reduced to such a state of bodily weakness that she could neither walk nor lie in bed.

She could only, night and day, sit in her chair; and having been confined for so many years in that posture, her limbs had become so stiff that any attempt to move her was attended with acute pain.

She was the mother-in-law of Samuel Matheson, and had, with her family, been removed by Mr Sellar from Rhimisdale some time before.

His treatment of her and others on that occasion had brought Mr Sellar into trouble, but now, in the Providence of God, she was once more in his power.

"Bean Raomasdail", or "the good wife of Rhimisdale", as she was called, was much revered.

When the evicting party commenced their operations in her township, the aged widow's house was among the very first that was to be consigned to the flames.

Her family and neighbours begged that she might be allowed to remain for only two days till a conveyance could be provided for her.

They were told that she should have thought on that before, and that she must immediately be removed by her friends, or the constables would be ordered to do it.

The good wife of Rhimisdale was, therefore, raised by her weeping family, from her chair and laid on a blanket, the corners of which were held up by four of the strongest youths in the place.

All this she bore with meekness, and while the eyes of her attendants were streaming with tears, her pale and gentle countenance was suffused with a smile.

The change of posture and the rapid motion of the bearers, however, awakened the most intense pain, and her cries never ceased till within a few miles of her destination, when she fell asleep.

A burning fever supervened, of which she died a few months later.

During these proceedings, I was resident at my father's house, but I had occasion on the week immediately ensuing to visit the manse of Tongue.

On my way thither, I passed through the scene of the campaign of burning. The spectacle presented was hideous and ghastly! The banks of the lake and the river, formerly studded with cottages, now met the eye as a scene of desolation.

Of all the houses, the thatched roofs were gone, but the walls, built of alternate layers of turf and stone, remained.

The flames of the preceding week still slumbered in their ruins, and sent up into the air spiral columns of smoke; whilst here a gable, and there a long side-wall, undermined by the fire burning within them, might be seen tumbling to the ground, from which a cloud of smoke, and then a dusky flame, slowly sprang up.

The sooty rafters of the cottages, as they were being consumed, filled the air with a heavy and most offensive smell.

In short, nothing could more vividly represent the horrors of grinding oppression, and the extent to which one man, dressed up in a "little brief authority", will exercise that power, without feeling or restraint, to the injury of his fellow-creatures.

Compensation for houses destroyed - a few pennies!

Dealing with the Sutherland Clearances General Stewart of Garth wrote in "Sketches of the Highlanders":

On the part of those who institute similar improvements, in which so few of the people were to have a share, conciliatory measures, and a degree of tenderness, beyond what would have been shown to strangers, were to have been expected towards the hereditary supporters of their families.

It was, however, unfortunately the natural consequences of the measures which were adopted, that few men of liberal feelings could be induced to undertake their execution.

The respectable gentlemen, who, in so many cases, had formerly been entrusted with the management of Highland property, resigned, and their places were supplied by persons cast in a coarser mould, and, generally, strangers to the country, who quickly surmounted every obstacle, and hurried on the change, without reflecting on the distress of which it might be productive.

To attempt a new system, and become acceptable tenants, required a little time and a little indulgence, two things which it was resolved should not be conceded them: they were immediately removed from the cultivated and fertile farms; some left the country, and others were offered limited portions of land on uncultivated moors, on which they were to form a settlement; and thus, while particular districts have been desolated, the gross numerical population has, in some manner, been preserved.

Many judicious men, however, doubt the policy of these measures, and dread their consequences on the condition and habits of the people.

This mode of sub-dividing small portions of inferior land is bad enough certainly, and to propose the establishment of villages, for the benefit of men who can neither betake themselves to the cultivation of the land nor to commerce for earning the means of subsistence, is doubtless a refinement in policy solely to be ascribed to the enlightened and enlarged views peculiar to the new system.

But, leaving out of view the consideration that, from the prevalence of turning corn lands into pasture, the demand for labour is diminished, while the number of labourers is increased, it can scarcely be expected that a man who had once been a farmer, possessed of land, and of considerable property in cattle, horses, sheep and money, should, without the most poignant feelings, descend to the rank of a hired labourer.

In the first removals of tenants, a small compensation (30 pence) in two separate sums, was allowed for the houses destroyed.

Some of the ejected tenants were also allowed small allotments of land, on which they were to build houses at their own expense, no assistance being given for that purpose.

Perhaps it was owing to this that they were the more reluctant to remove till they had built houses on their new stations.

The compensations allowed in the more recent removals are stated to have been more liberal; and the improvements which have succeeded those summary ejections of the ancient inhabitants are highly eulogised both in pamphlets and newspapers.

Some people may, however, be inclined to doubt the advantages of improvements which called for such frequent apologies; for, if more lenient measures had been pursued, vindication would have, perhaps, been unnecessary, and the trial of one of the acting agents might have been avoided

General Stewart adds the following in the third edition of his *Sketches,* published in 1825:-

The great changes which have taken place in the parishes of Sutherland, and some others, have excited a warm and general interest.

While the liberal expenditure of capital was applauded by all, many intelligent persons lamented that its application was so much in one direction; that the ancient tenantry were to have no share in this expenditure; and that so small a portion was allotted for the future settlement of the numerous population who had been removed from their farms, that great distress, disaffection, and hostility towards the landlords and government would be the inevitable result.

In autumn, 1823, I travelled over the "improved" districts, and a large portion of those parts which had been depopulated and laid out in extensive pastoral farms, as well as the stations in which the people are placed.

After as strict an examination as circumstances permitted, and a careful enquiry among those who, from their knowledge and judgment were enabled to form the best opinions, I do not find that I have one statement to alter, or one opinion to correct; though I am fully aware that many hold very different opinions.

But however much I may differ in some points, there is one in which I warmly and cordially join; and that is, in expressing my high satisfaction and admiration at the liberality displayed in the immense sums expended on buildings, in enclosing, clearing, and draining land, in forming roads and communications, and introducing the most improved agricultural implements.

Equally remarkable is the great abatement of rents given to the tenants of capital — abatements which it was not expected they would ask, considering the preference and encouragement given them, and the promises they had held out of great and unprecedented revenue, from their skill and exertions.

But these promises seem to have been early forgotten; the tenants of capital were the first to call for relief; and so great and generous has this relief been that the rents are reduced so low as to be almost on a level with what they were when the great changes commenced.

15,000 ejected in nine years — Sutherland's 'Irish style massacre'

*H*ugh Miller dealt with the Sutherland Clearances in "Sutherland as it was and Is". He wrote:

There appeared at Paris, about five years ago, a singularly ingenious work on political economy, from the pen of the late M de Sismondi, a writer of European reputation.

The greater part of the first volume is taken up with discussions on territorial wealth, and the condition of the cultivators of the soil; and in this portion of the work there is a prominent place assigned to a subject which perhaps few Scotch readers would expect to see introduced through the medium of a foreign tongue to the people of a great continental state.

We find this philosophic writer, whose works are known far beyond the limits of his language, devoting an entire essay to the case of the Duchess of Sutherland and her tenants, and forming a judgment on it very unlike the decision of political economists in our own country, who have not hesitated to characterise her great and singularly harsh experiment as at once justifiable in itself and happy in its results.

It is curious to observe how deeds done as if in darkness and in a corner, are beginning, after the lapse of nearly thirty years, to be proclaimed on the house tops.

The experiment of the late Duchess was not intended to be made in the eye of Europe. Its details would ill bear the exposure. When Cobbett simply referred to it, only ten years ago, the noble proprietrix was startled, as if a rather delicate family secret was on the eve of being divulged; and yet nothing seems more evident now than that civilized man all over the world is to be made aware of how the experiment was accomplished, and what it is ultimately to produce.

In a time of quiet and good order, the argument which the philosophic Frenchman employs on behalf of the ejected tenantry of Sutherland is an argument at which proprietors may afford to smile.

In a time of revolution, however, when lands change their owners, and old families give place to new ones, it might be found somewhat formidable — sufficiently so, at least, to lead a wise proprietor in an unsettled age rather to conciliate than oppress and irritate the class who would be able in such circumstances to urge it with most effect.

It is not easy doing justice in a few sentences to the facts and reasonings of an elaborate essay; but the line of argument runs thus:-

Under the old Celtic tenures — the only tenures, be it remembered through which the Lords of Sutherland derive their rights to their lands, — the *Klaan,* or children of the soil, were the proprietors of the soil — "the whole of Sutherland", says Sismondi, belonged to "the men of Sutherland".

Their chief was their monarch, and a very absolute monarch he was.

"He gave the different *tacks* of land to his officers, or took them away from them, according as they showed themselves more or less useful in war.

But though he could thus, in a military sense, reward or punish the clan, he could not diminish in the least the property of the clan itself;" — he was a chief, not a proprietor, and had "no more right to expel from their homes the inhabitants of his country, than a king to expel from his country the inhabitants of his kingdom".

"Now, the Gaelic tenant", continues the Frenchman, "has never been conquered; nor did he forfeit, on any after occasion, the rights which he originally possessed"; in point of right, he is still a co-proprietor with his captain.

To a Scotsman acquainted with the law of property as it has existed among us, even in the Highlands, for the last century, and everywhere else for at least two centuries more, the view may seem extreme; not so, however, to a native of the Continent, in many parts of which prescription and custom are found ranged, not on the side of the chief, but on that of the vassal.

"Switzerland", says Sismondi, "which in so many respects resembles Scotland, — in its lakes, its mountains, its climate, and the character, manners, and habits of its children, — was likewise at the same period parcelled out among a small number of lords.

If the Counts of Kyburgh, of Lentzburg, of Hapsburg, and of Gruyeres, had been protected by the English laws, they would find themselves at the present day precisely in the condition in which the Earls of Sutherland were twenty years ago.

Some of them would perhaps have had the same taste for *improvements*, and several republics would have been expelled from the Alps, to make room for flocks of sheep.

But while the law has given to the Swiss peasant a guarantee of perpetuity, it is to the Scottish laird that it has extended this guarantee in the British empire, leaving the peasant in a precarious situation.

The clan, — recognised at first by the captain, whom they followed in war, and obeyed for their common advantage, as his friends and relations, then as his soldiers, then as his vassal, then as his farmers, — he has come finally to regard as hired labourers, whom he may perchance allow to remain on the soil of their common country for his own advantage but whom he has the power to expel so soon as he no longer finds it for his interest to keep them".

Arguments like those of Sismondi, however much their force may be felt on the Continent, would be formidable at home, as we have said, in only a time of revolution, when the very foundations of society would be unfixed, and opinions set loose, to pull down or re-construct at pleasure.

But it is surely not uninteresting to mark how, in the course of events, that very law of England which, in the view of the Frenchman, has done the Highland peasant so much less, and the Highland chief so much more than justice, is bidding fair, in the case of Sutherland at least, to carry its rude equalising remedy along with it.

Between the years 1811 and 1820, fifteen thousand inhabitants of this northern district were ejected from their snug inland farms, by means for which we would in vain seek a precedent, except, perchance, in the history of the Irish massacre.

But though the interior of the county was thus improved into a desert, in which there are many thousands of sheep, but few human habitations, let it not be supposed by the reader that its general population was in any degree lessened.

So far was this from being the case, that the census of 1821 showed an increase over the census of 1811 of more than two hundred; and the present population of Sutherland exceeds, by a thousand, its population before the change.

The county has not been depopulated — its population has been merely arranged after a new fashion.

The late Duchess found it spread equally over the interior and the sea-coast, and in very comfortable circumstances; — she left it compressed into a wretched selvage of poverty and suffering that fringes the county on its eastern and western shores.

Why marriage of countess spelt disaster for locals

What was the economic condition of these Sutherland Highlanders? How did they fare?

The county had its less genial localities, in which, for a month or two in the summer season, when the stock of grain from the previous year was fast running out, and the crops on the ground not yet ripened for use, the people experienced a considerable degree of scarcity — such scarcity as a mechanic in the South feels when he has been a fortnight out of employment.

But the Highlander had resources in these seasons which the mechanic has not.

He had his cattle and his wild potherbs, such as the mug-wort and the nettle.

It has been adduced by the advocates of the change which has ruined Sutherland, as a proof of the extreme hardship of the Highlander's condition, that at such times he could have eaten as food broth made of nettles, mixed up with a little oatmeal, or have had resource to the expedient of bleeding his cattle, and making the blood into a sort of pudding.

And it is quite true that the Sutherlandshire Highlander was in the habit at such times, of having resource to such food.

It is not less true, however, that the statement is just as little conclusive regarding his condition, as if it were alleged that there must always be famine in France when the people eat the hind legs of frogs, or in Italy when they make dishes of snails.

With regard to the general comfort of the people in their old condition, there are better tests than can be drawn from the kind of food they occasionally ate.

The country hears often of dearth in Sutherland now. Every year in which the crop falls a little below average in other districts, is a year of famine there, but the country never heard of dearth in Sutherland then.

There were very few among the holders of its small inland farms who had not saved a little money. Their circumstances were such, that their moral nature found full room to develop itself, and in a way the world has rarely witnessed.

Never were there a happier or more contented people, or a people more strongly attached to the soil; and not one of them now lives in the altered circumstances on which they were so rudely precipitated by the landlord, who does not look back on this period of comfort and enjoyment with sad and hopeless regret.

But we have not yet said how this ruinous revolution was effected in Sutherland, — how the aggravations of the *mode*, if we may so speak, still fester in the recollections of the people, — or how thoroughly that policy of the lord of the soil, through which he now seems determined to complete the work of ruin which his predecessor began, harmonizes with its worst details.

We must first relate, however, a disastrous change which took place, in the providence of God, in the noble family of Sutherland, and which, though it dates fully eighty years back, may be regarded as pregnant with the disasters which afterwards befell the county.

The marriage of the young countess into a noble English family was fraught with further disaster to the county.

There are many Englishmen quite intelligent enough to perceive the difference between a smoky cottage of turf, and a whitewashed cottage of stone, whose judgments on their respective inhabitants would be of but little value.

Sutherland, as a county of men, stood higher at this period than perhaps any other district in the British Empire; but, as our descriptions have shown, it by no means stood high as a county of farms and cottages.

The marriage of the countess brought a new set of eyes upon it, — eyes accustomed to quite a different face of things. It seemed a wild, rude county, where all was wrong, and all had to be set right, — a sort of Russia on a small scale, that had just got another Peter the Great to civilize it, — or a sort of barbarous Egypt, with an energetic Ali Pasha at its head.

Even the vast wealth of the Stafford family militated against this hapless county.

It enabled them to treat it as a mere subject of an interesting experiment, in which gain to themselves was really no object, — nearly as little so, as if they had resolved on dissecting a dog alive for the benefit of science.

It was a still farther disadvantage, that they had to carry on their experiment by the hands, and to watch its first effects with the eyes, of others.

The agonies of the dog might have had their softening influence on a dissecter who held the knife himself; but there could be no such influence exerted over him, did he merely issue orders to his footman that the dissection should be completed, remaining himself, meanwhile, out of sight and out of hearing.

The plan of improvement sketched out by his English family was a plan exceedingly easy of conception. Here is a vast tract of land, furnished with two distinct sources of wealth.

Its shores may be made the seats of extensive fisheries, and the whole of its interior parcelled out into productive sheep farms.

All is waste in its present state; it has no fisheries, and two-thirds of its internal produce is consumed by the inhabitants.

It had contributed, for the use of the community and its landlord, its large herds of black cattle; but the English family saw, and, we believe, saw truly, that for every pound of beef which it produced, it could be made to produce two pounds of mutton, and perhaps a pound of fish in addition.

And it was resolved, therefore, that the inhabitants of the central districts, who, as they were mere Celts, could not be transformed, it was held, into store farmers, should be marched down to the sea-side, there to convert themselves into fishermen, on the shortest possible notice, and that a few farmers of capital, of the industrious Lowland race, should be invited to occupy the new sub-divisions of the interior.

And, pray, what objections can be urged against so liberal and large-minded a scheme?

The poor inhabitants of the interior had very serious objections to urge against it.

Their humble dwellings were of their own rearing; it was they themselves who had broken in their little fields from the waste; from time immemorial, far beyond the reach of history, had they possessed their mountain holdings, — they had defended them so well of old that the soil was still virgin ground, in which the invader had found only a grave; and their young men were now in foreign lands fighting at the command of their chieftain the battles of their country, not in the character of hired soldiers, but of men who regarded these very holdings as their stake in the quarrel.

To them, then, the scheme seemed fraught with the most flagrant, the most monstrous injustice.

The reader must keep in view, therefore, that if atrocities unexampled in Britain for at least a century were perpetrated in the clearing of Sutherland, there was a species of at least passive resistance on the part of the people (for active resistance there was none), which in some degree provoked them.

Had the Highlanders, on receiving orders, marched down to the sea-coast and become fishermen with the readiness with which a regiment deploys on review day, the atrocities would, we doubt not, have been much fewer.

But though the orders were very distinct, the Highlanders were very unwilling to obey; and the severities formed merely a part of the means through which the necessary obedience was ulitmately secured. We shall instance a single case as illustrative of the process.

In the month of March, 1814, a large proportion of the Highlanders of Farr and Kildonan, two parishes in Sutherland, were summoned to quit their farms in the following May.

In a few days after, the surrounding heath on which they pastured their cattle and from which, at that season, the sole supply of herbage is derived (for in those northern districts the grass springs late, and the cattle-feeder in the spring months depends chiefly on the heather), were set on fire and burned up.

There was that sort of policy in the stroke which men deem allowable in a state of war.

The starving cattle went roaming over the burnt pastures, and the greater part of what remained, though in miserable condition, the Highlanders had to sell perforce.

Most of the able-bodied men were engaged in this latter business at a distance from home, when the dreaded term day came on.

The pasturage had been destroyed before the legal term, and while in even the eye of the law it was still the property of the poor Highlanders; but ere disturbing them in their dwellings, term-day was suffered to pass.

The work of demolition then began.

A numerous party of men, with a factor at their head, entered the district, and commenced pulling down the houses over the heads of the inhabitants.

In an extensive tract of country not a human dwelling was left standing, and then, the more effectually to prevent their temporary re-erection, the destroyers set fire to the wreck.

In one day the people were deprived of home and shelter, and left exposed to the elements. Many deaths are said to have ensued from alarm, fatigue, and cold.

Dad carried sick children on his back for 25 miles

Let us follow, for a little, the poor Highlanders of Sutherland to the sea-coast.

It would be easy dwelling on the terrors of their expulsion, and multiplying facts of horror; but had there been no permanent deterioration effected in their condition, these, all harrowing and repulsive as they were, would have mattered less.

Sutherland would have soon recovered the burning-up of a few hunded hamlets, or the loss of a few bed-ridden old people, who would have died as certainly under cover, though perhaps a few months later, as when exposed to the elements in the open air.

Nay, had it lost a thousand of its best men in the way in which it lost so many at the storming of New Orleans, the blank ere now would have been completley filled up.

The calamaties of fire or of decimation even, however distressing in themselves, never yet ruined a country; no calamity ruins a country that leaves the surviving inhabitants to develop, in their old circumstances, their old character and resources.

In one of the eastern eclogues of Collins, where two shepherds are described as flying for their lives before the troops of a ruthless invader, we see with how much of the terrible the imagination of a poet could invest the evils of war, when aggravated by pitiless barbarity.

Fertile as that imagination was, however, there might be found new circumstances to heighten the horrors of the scene — circumstances beyond the reach of invention — in the retreat of the Sutherland Highlanders from the smoking ruins of their cottages to their allotments on the coast.

We have heard of one man, named Mackay, whose family at the time of the greater conflagration referred to by Macleod, were all lying ill of fever, who had to carry two of his sick children on his back a distance of twenty-five miles.

We have heard of the famished people blackening the shores, like the crew of some vessel wrecked on an inhospitable coast, that they might sustain life by the shell-fish and sea-weed laid bare by the ebb.

Many of their allotments, especially on the western coast, were barren in the extreme — unsheltered by bush or tree, and exposed to the sweeping sea-winds, and in time of tempest, to the blighting spray; and it was found a matter of the extremest difficulty to keep the few cattle which they had retained, from wandering into the better sheltered and more fertile interior.

The poor animals were intelligent enough to read a practical comment on the nature of the change effected; and, from the harshness of the shepherds to whom the care of the interior had been entrusted, they served materially to add to the distress of their unhappy masters. They were getting continually impounded; and vexatious fines, in the form of trespass-money, came thus to be wrung from the already impoverished Highlanders.

Many who had no money to give were obliged to relieve them by depositing some of their few portable articles of value, such as bed or body clothes, or, more distressing still, watches, and rings, and pins — the only relics, in not a few instances, of brave men whose bones were mouldering under the fatal rampart at New Orleans, or in the arid sands of Egypt — on that spot of proud recollection, where the invincibles of Napoleon went down before the Highland bayonet.

Their first efforts as fishermen were what might be expected from a rural people unaccustomed to the sea.

The shores of Sutherland, for immense tracts together, are iron-bound, and much exposed.

There could not be more perilous seas for the unpractised boatman to take his first lessons on; but though the casualties were numerous and the loss of life great, many of the younger Highlanders became expert fishermen.

The experiment was harsh in the extreme, but so far, at least, it succeeded.

It lies open, however, to other objections than those which have been urged against it on the score of its inhumanity.

Why changes were needed — by Sutherland estates man

In An Account of the Improvements on the Estates of the Marquis of Stafford published in 1821 James Kinloch, General Agent of the Sutherland Estates wrote:-

No country of Europe at any period of its history ever presented more formidable obstacles to the improvement of a people arising out of the prejudices and feelings of the people themselves.

To the tacksman, it is clear, from what has already been stated, such a change could not be agreeable ...

Its effect being to alter his condition, and remove him from a state of idle independence to a situation in which his livelihood was to be obtained by his exertions and industry.

Nor could it be agreeable to him to lose that command

and influence, which he had hitherto exercised without control, over his sub-tenants and dependants; while it was at variance with every feeling and prejudice in which he had been brought up and educated.

It required minds of no ordinary cast to rise superior to these feelings; and men of no common understanding and vigour of intellect were required, to shake off habits so opposed to active industry and exertion.

From a certain set of this class, therefore, a real and determined opposition to any change was to be looked for.

This expectation has not been disappointed; and it is from individuals of this class, and persons connected with them, that those false and malignant representations have proceeded, which have been so loudly and extensively circulated.

Actuated by motives of a mere personal nature they attempted to make an appeal in favour of a set of people who were never before the objects of their commiseration, in order that they might reduce them to that state of degredation from which they had been just emancipated.

This was, however, by no means true of the whole, or of the greater part of this class of gentlemen; for the bulk of the most active improvers of Sutherland are natives, who, both as sheep farmers, and as skilful and enterprising agriculturalists, are equal to any to be met with in the kingdom.

They have, with an intelligence and liberality of feeling embraced with alacrity the new scene of active exertion presented for their adoption; seconding the views of the landlords with the utmost zeal, marked with much foresight and prudence.

Out of the twenty-nine principal tacksmen of the estate, seventeen are natives of Sutherland, four are Northumbrians, two are from the county of Moray, two from Roxburghshire, two from Caithness, one from Midlothian, and one from the Merse.

So strong, however, were the prejudices of the people, that, even to those who were subjected to the power and control of the tacksmen, this mode of life had charms which attached them strongly to it.

He extended, in some degree, to the more respectable of those who were placed under him, the same familiarity which he received from the chief.

The burden of the outdoor work was cast upon the females. The men deemed such an occupation unworthy of them, continued labour of any sort being most averse to their habits.

They were contented with the most simple and the poorest fare.

Like all mountaineers, accustomed to a life of irregular exertion, with intervals of sloth, they were attached with a degree of enthusiasm, only felt by the natives of a poor country, to their own glen and mountainside, adhering in the strongest manner to the habits and homes of their fathers.

They deemed no comfort worth the possessing, which was to be purchased at the price of regular industry; no improvement worthy of adoption, if it was to be obtained at the expense of sacrificing the customs, or leaving the homes of their ancestors.

So strongly did these feelings operate, that it cost them nearly the same effort to remove from the spot in which they were born and brought up, though the place of their new dwelling was situated on the sea-shore at the mouth of their native strath as it cost them to make an exertion equal to transporting themselves across the Atlantic.

The cattle which they reared on the mountains, and from the sale of which they depended for the payment of their rents, were of the poorest description.

During summer they procured a scanty sustenance, with much toil and labour, by roaming over the mountains; while in winter they died in numbers for the want of support; notwithstanding a practice, which they universally adopted, of killing every second calf, on account of the want of winter keep.

To such an extent did this calamity at times amount, that, in the spring of 1807, there died in the parish of Kildonan alone, two hundred cows, five hundred head of cattle, and more than two hundred small horses.

As soon as the works, undertaken under the direction of the Parliamentary Commissioners, opened a prospect of removing successfully the obstacles which stood in the way of the improvements of the people, steps were taken to new model and arrange these extensive possessions.

The utmost caution and deliberation was used in doing so, and plans were never more maturely weighed, nor executed with more anxiety and tenderness.

It is well known that the borders of Scotland and England were inhabited by a numerous population, who, in their pursuits, manners and general structure of society, bore a considerable resemblance to that which existed in the Highlands of Scotland.

When the union of the crowns rendered the maintenance of that irregular population unnecessary, the people were removed, and the mountains were covered with sheep.

Therefore it had been for a length of time proved by the experience of the stock farmers of those mountain tracts, which comprise the northern districts of England, and the southern parts of Scotland, that such situations were peculiarly suited for the maintenance of this species of stock.

Taking this example as their guide, experience had still further proved, that the central and western Highlands of Scotland were equally well calculated for the same end.

Reasoning from this success, and observing that the climate of Sutherland, owing to its vicinity to the ocean, and to its being considerably intersected by arms of the sea, was much more moderate than this latter district, it was fairly concluded that this county was even better fitted for this system of management, than the heights of Perthshire and Inverness-shire.

The inferior elevation of its mountains contributed still further to this effect, and held out every encouragement to adopt the same course which had been pursued with such success in both parts of the kingdom.

The succession of those Alpine plants, which are common to the Cheviot Hills, when they are put under sheep, being also the natural herbage of the mountains of Sutherland, renders them still more suitable to this mode of occupation.

On the first melting of the snow, the cotton grass is found to have been growing rapidly; it forms a healthy and an abundant food for sheep, until about the beginning of May, at which time it is in seed; when, after a short interval, the deer hair takes its place, starting up almost instantaneously, and forming, in the course of one week (if the ground has been recently burnt, and the weather be favourable), a green cover to the mountains.

This plant grows with several varieties of bents, until the end of July, when the cotton grass again begins to spring, and with the pry moss, comes a second time into flower, in September, after which the heather and more heating plants continue until the frosts of winter.

Nor is there any part of these mountains, over which the sheep cannot roam with ease, in search of food, rendering the whole available and profitable.

As there was every reason therefore for concluding, that the mountainous parts of the estate and indeed of the county of Sutherland, were as much calculated for the maintenance of stock as they were unfit for the habitation of man, there could be no doubt as to the propriety of converting them into sheep walks, *provided* the people could be at the same time settled in situations, where they could obtain a decent livelihood, and not be exposed to the recurrence of those privations, which so frequently and terribly afflicted them, when situated among the mountains.

It was a matter of important consideration, to determine how this was to be accomplished.

The local peculiarities of the county presented none of those advantages in disposing of, and absorbing the surplus population, which the borders of the two kingdoms, and the southern and eastern highlands had enjoyed.

Besides it had made no approximation to the state in which the rest of Scotland was placed, when those changes were carried into effect. It had stood still in the midst of that career of improvement which had so remarkably and so splendidly distinguished the rest of the kingdom; and remained separated by its habits, prejudices, and language, from all around.

It had long been known, that the coast of Sutherland abounded with many different kinds of fish, not only sufficient for the consumption of the country, but affording also a supply *to any extent*, for more distant markets or for exportation, when cured and salted.

Besides the regular and continual supply of white fish, with which the shores thus abound, the coast of Sutherland is annually visited by one of those vast shoals of herrings, which frequent the coast of Scotland.

It seemed as if it had been pointed out by Nature, that the system for this remote district, in order that it might bear its suitable importance in contributing its share to the general stock of the country, was, to convert the mountainous districts into sheep walks, and to remove the inhabitants to the coast, or to the valleys near the sea.

It will be seen, that the object to be obtained by this arrangement, was two-fold; it was, in the first place, to render this mountainous district contributory, as far as it was possible, to the general wealth and industry of the country, and in the manner most suitable to its situation and peculiar circumstances.

This was to be effected by making it produce a large supply of wool, for the staple manufactory of England.

At the same time, it should support as numerous, and a far more laborious and useful population, than it hitherto had done at home: and, in the second place, convert the inhabitants of those districts to the habits of regular and continued industry, and to enable them to bring to market a very considerable surplus quantity of provisions, for the supply of the large towns in the southern parts of the island or for the purpose of exportation.

A policy well calculated to raise the importance, and increase the happiness of the individuals themselves, who were the objects of the change, to benefit those to whom these extensive but hitherto unproductive possessions belonged, and to promote the general prosperity of the nation: such was the system which was adopted.

In carrying it into effect, every care was taken to explain the object proposed to be accomplished, to those who were to be removed, and to point out to them, the ultimate advantages that would necessarily accrue to them, from their completion.

These communications were made to the people by the factor personally, or by written statements, communicated to them by the ground officers.

That nothing might be omitted in this respect, the different ministers, and the principal tacksmen connected with the districts which were to be newly arranged, were written to, explaining to them, fully and explicitly, the intentions of the proprietors in adopting them.

It was particularly requested of these gentlemen, that they would impress upon the minds of the people, the propriety of agreeing to them, and of explaining, that the motives which dictated this step, arose out of a real regard for their interests and prosperity, as well as for the general improvement of the estate.

These representations had the desired effect, and nothing can be more praiseworthy, or deserve more to be applauded, than the conduct of the people on quitting their original habitations; for although they left them with much regret, they did so in the most quiet, orderly, and peaceable manner.

If, upon one occasion, in the earlier years of these arrangements, a momentary feeling of a contrary nature was exhibited, it arose entirely from the misconduct of persons whose duty it was to have recommended and enforced obedience to the laws, in place of infusing into the minds of the people, feelings of a contrary description.

As soon, however, as the interference of these persons was withdrawn, the poor people returned to their usual state of quietness and repose.

All the statements, giving a different acount of their conduct, are absolutely false, and a libel upon their good conduct and peaceable character.

These arrangements commenced in 1807, and have been carried on from that period, as the different tacks expired, and afforded an opportunity of doing so.

Bad years and the failure of crops continued to produce the same miserable effects they had constantly occasioned on that portion of the population which still continued to reside amongst the mountains.

This calamity fell with great severity upon them in the seasons of 1812-13 and 1816-17.

In order to alleviate misery every exertion was made by Lord Stafford. To those who had cattle he advanced money to the amount of above three thousand pounds.

To supply those who had no cattle, he sent meal into the country to the amount of nearly nine thousand pounds.

Besides which, Lady Stafford distributed money to each parish on the estate: in order that no pains nor consideration might be wanting, it was arranged that the gentleman who is at the head of his Lordship's affairs, the writer of this statement, should go to Dunrobin to settle with the local management and the clergymen, what was the best and most effectual way of distributing his Lordship's relief. Similar means were taken by Lord Reay, to alleviate the distresses of his people.

While such was the distress of those who still remained among the hills, *it was hardly felt by those who had settled upon the coast.*

Their new occupation. as fishermen, rendered them not only independent of that which produced the misery of their neighbours, but enabled them at the same time, in some degree, to become contributors towards their support, both by the fish they were able to sell to them, and also by the regular payment of their rents.

For it need hardly be stated that these wretched sufferers not only required to be relieved but failed entirely in the payment of what they owed the landlord.

Forced to live in a graveyard — despair of Ross-shire families

Great cruelties were perpetrated at Glencalvie, Ross-shire, where the evicted had to retire into the parish churchyard.

There for more than a week they found the only shelter obtainable in their native land. No one dared to succour them, under a threat of receiving similar treatment to those whose hard fate had driven them thus among the tombs.

Many of them, indeed, wished that their lot had landed them under the sod with their ancestors and friends, rather than be treated and driven out of house and home in such a ruthless manner.

A special commissioner sent down by the London **Times** describes the circumstances as follows:-

ARDGAY, NEAR TAIN, ROSS-SHIRE
15th May, 1845

Those who remember the misery and destitution to which large masses of the population were thrown by the systematic "Clearances" (as they are here called) carried on in Sutherland some 20 years ago, will regret to learn the heartless scourge with all its sequences of misery, of destitution, and of crime, is again being resorted to in Ross-shire.

Amongst an imaginative people like the Highlanders, it requires little, with fair treatment, to make them almost idolise their heritor.

They would spend the last drop of their blood in his service. But this feeling of respectful attachment to the landowners, which money cannot buy, is fast passing away.

This change is not without cause, as peasants are driven out from the means of self-support, to become wanderers and starving beggars.

One of these clearances is about to take place in the parish of Kincardine, from which I now write; and throughout the whole district it has created the strongest feeling of indignation.

This parish is divided into two districts each of great extent; one is called the parliamentary district of Croik.

The length of this district is about 20 miles, with a breadth of from 10 to 15 miles.

It extends amongst the most remote and unfrequented parts of the country, consisting chiefly of hills of heather and rock, peopled only in a few straths and glens.

This district was formerly thickly peopled; but one of those clearances many years ago nearly swept away the population, and now the whole number of its inhabitants amounts, I am told, to only 370 souls.

These are divided into three straths or glens, and live in a strath called Amatnatua, another strath called Greenyard, and in Glencalvie.

It is the inhabitants of Glencalvie, in number 90 people, whose turn it is now to be turned out of their homes, all at once, the aged and the helpless as well as the young and strong; nearly the whole of them without hope or prospects for the future.

The proprietor of this glen is Major Charles Robertson of Kindeace, who is at present out with his regiment in Australia; and his factor or steward who acts for him in his absence is Mr James Gillanders of Highfield Cottage, near Dingwall.

Glencalvie is situated about 25 miles from Tain, eastward. Bleak rough hills, whose surface are almost all rock and heather, closed in on all sides, leaving in the valley a gentle declivity of arable land of a very poor description, dotted over by cairns of stone and rock, not, at the utmost computation, of more than 15 to 20 acres in extent.

For this piece of indifferent land with a right of pasturage on the hills impinging upon it the almost incredible rent of £55.10s. has been paid. I am convinced that for the same land no farmer in England would give £15 at the utmost.

Even respectable farmers here say they do not know how the people raise the rent for it. Potatoes and barley were grown in the valley, and some sheep and a few black cattle find provender amongst the heather.

Eighteen families have each a cottage in the valley; they have always paid their rent punctually, and they have contrived to support themselves in all ordinary seasons.

They have no poor on the poor roll, and they help one another over the winter. I am told that not an inhabitant of this valley has been charged with any offence for years back.

During the war it furnished many soldiers; and an old pensioner, 82 years of age, who has served in India, is now dying in one of these cottages, where he was born.

For the convenience of the proprietor, some ten years ago, four of the principal tenants became bound for the rest, to collect all the rents and pay the whole in one sum.

The Lord Advocate has attempted to justify this clearance by writing that shortly after Mr Gillanders assumed the management of Major Robertson's estate, he found that it became absolutely necessary to adopt a different system, in regard to the lands of Glencalvie, "from that hitherto pursued".

The "different system" as it appears was to turn the barley and potato grounds into a sheep walk, and the "absolute necessity" for it is an alleged increase of rent.

It was accordingly, in 1843, attempted to serve summonses of removal upon the tenants. They were in no arrears of rent, they had no burdens in poor; for 500 years their fathers had peaceably occupied the glen, and the people were naturally indignant.

Who can be surprised that, on the constables going amongst them with the summonses, they acted in a manner which, while it showed their excitement, not the less evinced their wish to avoid breaking the law?

The women met the constables beyond the boundaries, over the river, and seized the hand of the one who held the notices; whilst some held it out by the wrist, others held a live coal to the papers and set fire to them.

They were afraid of being charged with destroying the notices, and they sought thus to evade the consequences. This act of resistance on their part has been made the most of.

One of the men told me, hearing they were to be turned out because they did not pay rent enough, that they offered to pay £15 a year more, and afterwards to pay as much rent as any other man would give for the place.

The following year (1844), however, the four chief tenants were decoyed to Tain, under the assurance that Mr Gillanders was going to settle, but instead notice to quit was given.

Having been served, "a decreet of removal" was obtained, under which, if they refused to turn out they would be put out by force.

Finding themselves in this position, they entered into an arrangement with Mr Gillanders, in which after several propositions on either side, it was agreed that they should remain until the 12th of May, to give them time to provide themselves with holdings elsewhere, Mr Gillanders agreeing to pay them £100 on quitting, and to take their stock on at a valuation.

They were also to have liberty to carry away the timber of their houses, which was really worthless, except for firewood.

On their part they agreed to leave peaceably, and not to lay down any crop.

Beyond the excessive harshness of removing the people at all, it is but right to say that the mode of proceeding in the removal hitherto has been temperate and considerate.

Two respectable farmers became bound for the people that they would carry out their part of the agreement, and the time of removal has since been extended to the 25th of this month.

In the defence got up for this proceeding it is stated that all have been provided for; this is not only not the case, but seems to be intentionally deceptive.

In speaking of all, the four principal tenants only are meant; for, according to the factor, these were all he had to do with; but this is not the case even in regard to the four principal tenants.

Two only, a father and son, have got a piece of black moor, near Tain, 25 miles off, without any house or shed on it, out of which they hope to obtain subsistence.

For this they are to pay £1 rent for 7 acres the first year; £2 for the second year; and £3 for a continuation.

Another old man with a family has got a house and a small lot of land in Edderton, about 20 miles off.

The old pensioner, if removing does not kill him, has obtained for himself and his family, a house at a rent of £3 or £4, some ten miles off, without any land or means of subsistence attached to it.

This old soldier has been offered 2s. a week by the factor to support him while he lives.

He was one of the four principal tenants bound for the rent; and he indignantly refuses to be kept as a pauper.

A widow with four children, two imbecile, has obtained two small apartments in a bothy or turf hut near Bonar

Bridge, for which she is to pay £2 rent, without any land or means of subsistence.

Another, a man with a wife and four children, has got an apartment at Bonar Bridge, at £1 rent. He goes there quite destitute, without means of living.

Six only of eighteen households, therefore, have been able to obtain places in which to put their heads; and of these, three only have any means of subsistence before them. The rest are hopeless and helpless.

Two or three of the men told me they have been round to every factor and proprietor in the neighbourhood, and they could obtain no place, and nothing to do, and they did not know where to go, or what to do to live.

Let me add that so far from the clearance at Glencalvie being a solitary instance in this neighbourhood, it is one of many.

The tenants of Newmore, near Tain, who I am told, amount to 16 families, are to be weeded out (as they express it here) on the 25th, by the same Mr Gillanders. The same factor manages the Strathconon estate, about 30 miles from Newmore, from which during the last four years, some hundreds of families have been weeded.

The Government Church of that district, built eighteen years ago, to meet the necessities of the population, is now almost unnecessary from the want of population.

At Black Isle, near Dingwall, the same agent is pursuing the same course, and so strong is the feeling of the poor Highlanders at these outrageous proceedings, that it is owing to the influence of religion alone that they refrain from breaking out into open and turbulent resistance of the law.

Grass and earth were dyed red with blood

In a "Sermon for the Times", the Rev. Richard Hibbs of the Episcopal Church, Edinburgh, referring to these evictions, says:— "Take first, the awful proof how far in oppression men can go — men highly educated and largely gifted in every way — property, talents, all; for the most part indeed, they are so-called noblemen.

What, then, are they doing in the Highland districts, according to the testimony of a learned professor in this city?

Why, depopulating those districts in order to make room for red deer. And how? By buying off the cottars, and giving them money to emigrate?

Not at all, but by starving them out; by rendering them absolutely incapable of procuring subsistence for themselves and families; for they first take away from them their apportionments of poor lands, although they may have paid their rents; and if that doesn't suffice to eradicate from their hearts that love of the soil on which they have been born and bred these inhuman landlords take away from the poor cottars the very roof above their defenceless heads, and expose them to the inclemencies of a northern sky; and this, forsooth, because they must have plenty room for their dogs and deer.

For plentiful instances of the most wanton barbarities under this head we need only point to the Knoydart evictions. Here were perpetrated such enormities as might well have caused the very sun to hide his face at noon-day".

The reader, utterly appalled by these horrifying statements, finds it difficult to retain the recollection that he is perusing the history of his own times, and country too.

He would fain yield himself to the tempting illusion that the ruthless atrocities which are depicted were enacted in a fabulous period, in ages long past; or some far distant, uncivilized region of our globe.

But alas! it is Scotland, in the latter half of the nineteenth century, of which he reads.

One feature of the heart-harrowing case is the cruelty that was practised on this occasion upon the female portion of the evicted clan.

Mr D Ross, in a letter addressed to the Right Hon. the Lord Advocate, Edinburgh, dated April 19, 1854, writes in reference to one of those clearances and evictions which had just then taken place, under the authority of a certain Sheriff of the district, and by means of a body of policemen as executioners:— "The feeling on this subject, not only in the district, but in Sutherlandshire and Ross-shire, is, among the great majority of the people, one of universal condemnation of the Sheriff's reckless conduct, and of indignation and disgust at the brutality of the policemen.

Such, indeed, was the sad havoc made on the females on the banks of the Carron, on the memorable 31st March last, that pools of blood were upon the ground — that the grass and earth were dyed red with it — that the dogs of the district came and licked up the blood; and at last, such was the state of feeling of parties who went from a distance to see the field, that a party (it is understood by order or instructions from headquarters) actually harrowed the ground during the night to hide the blood!

The affair at Greenyard, on the morning of the 31st March last, is not calculated to inspire much love of country, or rouse the martial spirit of the already ill-used Highlanders.

The savage treatment of innocent females on that morning, by an enraged body of police, throws the Sinope butchery into the shade; for the Ross-shire Haynaus have shown themselves more cruel and more blood-thirsty than the Austrian women-floggers.

What could these poor men and women — with their wounds and scars, and broken bones, and disjointed arms, stretched on beds of sickness, or moving on crutches, the result of the brutal treatment of them by the police at Greenyard — have to dread from the invasion of Scotland by Russia?' "

Commenting on this incredible atrocity, committed in the middle of the nineteenth century, Donld Macleod says truly that:— "It was so horrifying and so brutal that he did not wonder at the rev. gentleman's delicacy in speaking of it, and directing his hearers to peruse Mr Ross's pamphlet for full information".

Mr Ross went from Glasgow to Greenyard to investigate the case upon the spot, and found that Mr Taylor, a native of Sutherland, well educated in the evicting schemes and murderous cruelty of that county, and Sheriff-substitute of Ross-shire, marched from Tain upon the morning of the 31st March, at the head of a strong party of armed constables, with heavy bludgeons and fire-arms, conveyed in carts and other vehicles. They were allowed as much drink as they chose to take so as to qualify them for the bloody work which they had to perform; fit for any outrage, fully equipped, and told by the Sheriff to show no mercy to any one who would oppose them.

In this excited, half-drunken state, they came in contact with the unfortunate women of Greenyard, who were determined to prevent the officers from serving the summonses of removal upon them, and keep the holding of small farms where they and their forefathers lived and died for generations.

But no time was allowed for parley; the Sheriff gave the order to clear the way, and, be it said to his everlasting disgrace, he struck the first blow at a woman, the mother of a large family, and large in the family way at the time, who tried to keep him back; then a general slaughter commenced; the women made noble resistance, until the bravest of them got their arms broken; then they gave way.

This did not allay the rage of the murderous brutes, they continued clubbing at the protectless creatures until every one of them was stretched on the field, weltering in their blood, or with broken arms, ribs, and bruised limbs.

In this woeful condition many of them were hand-cuffed together, others tied with coarse ropes, huddled into carts, and carried prisoners to Tain.

I have seen myself in the possession of Mr Ross, Glasgow, patches or scalps of the skin with the long hair adhering to them, which was found upon the field a few days after this inhuman affray.

I did not see the women, but I was told that gashes were found on the heads of two young female prisoners in Tain jail, which exactly corresponded with the slices of scalps which I have seen, so that Sutherland and Ross-shire may boast of having had the Nana Sahib and his chiefs some few years before India.

Mr Donald Ross placed the whole affair before the Lord Advocate for Scotland, but no notice was taken of it by that functionary, further than that the majesty of the law would need to be observed and attended to.

From the same estate (the estate of Robertson of Kindeace, if I am not mistaken in the date) in the year 1843 the whole inhabitants of Glencalvie were evicted in a similar manner, and so unprovided and unprepared were they for removal at such an inclement season of the year, that they had to shelter themselves in a Church and a burying-ground.

I have seen myself nineteen families within this gloomy and solitary resting abode of the dead. They were there for months.

In the year 1819 or '20, about the time when the depopulation of Sutherland was completed, and the annual conflagration of burning the houses ceased, a sheep farmer from there fixed his eyes upon a glen in Ross-shire, inhabited by a brave, hardy race from time immemorial.

Summonses of removal were served upon them at once. The people resisted — a military force was brought against them — the military and the women of the glen met at the entrance to the glen, and a bloody conflict took place; without reading the riot act or taking any other precaution, the military fired (by the order of Sheriff MacLeod) ball cartridge upon the women; one young girl of the name of Mathieson was shot dead on the spot; many were wounded.

When this murder was observed by the survivors, and some young men concealed in the background, they made a heroic sudden rush upon the military, when a hand-to-hand melee or fight took place.

In a few minutes the military were put to disorder by flight; in their retreat they were unmercifully dealt with, only two of them escaping with whole heads.

The Sheriff's coach was smashed to atoms, and he made a narrow escape himself with a whole head.

But no legal cognizance was taken of this affair, as the Sheriff and the military were the violators.

However, for fear of prosecution, the Sheriff settled a pension of £6 sterling yearly upon the murdered girl's father, and the case was hushed up likewise.

The result was that the people kept possession of the glen, and that the proprietor and the oldest and most insatiable of Sutherland scourges went to law, which ended in the ruination of the latter, who died a pauper".

Hugh Miller, describing a "Highland Clearing", in one of his able leading articles in the *Witness*, since published in volume form, quotes freely from an article by John Robertson, which appeared in the *Glasgow National* in August, 1844, on the evictions of the Rosses of Glencalvie.

When the article from which Hugh Miller quotes was written, the inhabitants of the glen had just received notices of removal, but the evictions had not yet been carried out.

Commenting on the proceedings Hugh Miller says:—

"In an adjacent glen (to Strathcarron) a summons of removal has been served within the last few months on a whole community."

Angry women battle against Sheriff's men — 15 badly hurt

The constitution of society in the Glen, says Mr Robertson, is remarkably simple. Four heads of families are bound for the whole rental.

The number of souls was about ninety, sixteen cottages paid rent; they supported a teacher for the education of their own children; they supported their own poor.

"The laird has never lost a farthing of rent in bad years, such as 1836 and 1837, the people may have required the favour of a few weeks' delay, but they are not now a single farthing in arrears;" that is, when they are in receipt of summonses of removal.

"For a century", Mr Robertson continues, speaking of the Highlanders, "their privileges have been lessening; they dare not now hunt the deer, or shoot the grouse or the blackcock; they have no longer the range of the hills for their cattle and their sheep; they must not catch a salmon in the stream; in earth, air, and water, the rights of the laird are greater, and the rights of the people are smaller, than they were in the days of their forefathers".

The same writer eloquently concludes:—

"The father of the laird of Kindeace bought Glencalvie. It was sold by a Ross two short centuries ago. The swords of the Rosses of Glencalvie did their part in protecting this little glen, as well as the broad lands of Pitcalvie, from the ravages and clutches of hostile septs.

These clansmen bled and died in the belief that every principle of honour and morals secured their descendants a right to subsisting on the soil.

The chiefs and their children had the same charter of the sword.

Some Legislatures have made the right of the people superior to the right of the chief; British law-makers made the rights of the chief everything, and those of their followers nothing.

The ideas of the morality of property are in most men the creatures of their interests and sympathies.

Of this there cannot be a doubt, however, the chiefs would not have had the land at all, could the clansmen have foreseen the present state of the Highlands — their children in mournful groups going into exile — the faggot of legal myrmidons in the thatch of the feal cabin — the hearths of their homes and their lives in the green sheep-walks of the stranger.

Sad it is, that it is seemingly the will of our constituencies that our laws shall prefer the few to the many.

Most mournful will it be, should the clansmen of the Highlands have been cleared away, ejected, exiled, in deference to a political, a moral, a social, and an economical mistake — a suggestion not of philosophy, but of mammon — a system in which the demon of sordidness assumed the shape of the angel of civilization and light."

That the Eviction of the Rosses was of a harsh character is amply corroborated by the following account, extracted from the *Inverness Courier*:—

"At six o'clock on the morning of Friday last, Sheriff Taylor proceeded from Tain, accompanied by several Sheriff's officers, and a police force of about thirty.

On arriving at Greenyards, which is nearly four miles from Bonar Bridge, it was found that about three hundred persons, fully two-thirds of whom were women, had assembled from the county round about, all apparently prepared to resist the execution of the law.

The women stood in front, armed with stones, and the men occupied the background, all, or nearly all, furnished with sticks.

The Sheriff attempted to reason with the crowd, and to show them the necessity of yielding to the law: but his efforts were fruitless; and he was reluctantly obliged to employ force.

After a sharp resistance, which happily lasted only a few minutes, the people were dispersed, and the Sheriff was enabled to execute the summonses upon the four tenants.

The women, as they bore the brunt of the battle, were the principal sufferers. A large number of them — fifteen or sixteen, we believe, were seriously hurt, and of these several are under medical treatment; one woman, we believe, still lies in a precarious condition.

The policemen appear to have used their batons with great force, but they escaped themselves almost unhurt.

Several correspondents from the district complain that the policemen used their batons with wanton cruelty.

Others state that they not only did their duty, but that less firmness might have proved fatal to themselves.

The instances of violence are certainly, though very naturally, on the part of the attacking force; several batons were smashed in the melee; a great number of men and women were seriously hurt, especially about the head and face, while not one of the policemen, so far as we can learn, suffered any injury in consequence.

As soon as the mob was fairly dispersed, the police made active pursuit, in the hope of catching some of the ringleaders.

The men had, however, fled, and the only persons apprehended were some women, who had been active in the opposition, and who had been wounded.

They were conveyed to the prison at Tain, but liberated on bail next day, through the intercession of a gallant friend, who became responsible for their appearance".

"A correspondent writes", continues the *Courier*, "ten young women were wounded in the back of the skull and other parts of their bodies ... The wounds on these women show plainly the severe manner in which they were dealt with by the police when they were retreating.

It was currently reported last night that one of them was dead; and the feeling of indignation is so strong against the manner in which the constables have acted, that I fully believe the life of any stranger, if he were supposed to be an officer of the law, would not be worth twopence in the district".

How land grabbers got their just deserts

During the first years of the century a great many were cleared from KINTAIL by Seaforth, at the instigation of his sheep farmer factor.

In Glengarry, Canada, a few years ago, we met one man, 93 years of age, who was among the evicted.

He was in excellent circumstances, his three sons having three valuable farms of their own, and considered wealthy in the district.

In the same county there is a large colony of Kintail men, the descendants of those cleared from that district, all comfortable, many of them very well off, one of them being then member for his county in the dominion Parliament.

While this has been the case with many of the evicted fom Kintail and their descendants in Canada, the grasping sheep farmer who was the original cause of their eviction from their native land, died ruined and penniless; and the Seaforths, not long after, had to sell the last inch of their ancient inheritance in Lochalsh and Kintail.

The attempt to evict the COIGEACH crofters must also be mentioned. Here the people made a stout resistance, the women disarming about twenty policemen and sheriff-officers, burning the summonses in a heap, throwing their batons into the sea, and ducking the representatives of the law in a neighbouring pool.

The men formed the second line of defence, in case the women should receive any ill-treatment.

They, however, never put a finger on the officers of the law, all of whom returned home without serving a single summons or evicting a single crofter.

The proceedings of her subordinates fortunately came to the ears of the noble proprietrix, with the result that the Coigeach tenants are still where they were, and are today among the most comfortable crofters in the north of Scotland.

From 1840 to 1848 STRATHCONON was almost entirely cleared of its ancient inhabitants to make room for sheep and deer, as in other places; and also for the purposes of extensive forest plantations.

The property was under trustees when the harsh proceedings were commenced by the factor, Mr Rose, a notorious Dingwall solicitor.

He began by taking away, first, the extensive hill-pasture, for generations held as club-farms by the townships, thus reducing the people from a position of comfort and independence; and secondly, as we saw done elsewhere, finally evicting them from the arable portion of the strath, though they were not a single penny in arrear of rent.

Coirre-Bhuic and Scard-Roy were first cleared, and given, respectively, as sheep-farms to Mr Brown, from Moray-shire, and Colin Munro, from Dingwall.

Mr Balfour, when he came of age, cleared Coire-Feola and Achadh-an-eas;; Carnach was similarly treated, while no fewer than twenty-seven families were evicted from Glen-Meine alone.

Baile-a-Mhuilinn and Baile-na-Creige were cleared in 1844, no fewer than twenty-four families from these townships removing to the neighbourhood of Knock-farrel and Loch Ussie, above Dingwall, where they were provided with holdings by the late John Hay Mackenzie of Cromartie, father of the present Duchess of Sutherland, and where a few of themselves and many of their descendants are now in fairly comfortable circumstances.

A great many more found shelter on various properties in the Black Isle — some at Drynie Park, Maol-Bui; others at Kilcoy, Allangrange, Cromarty, and the Aird.

It is computed that from four to five hundred souls were thus driven from Strathconon, and cast adrift on the world, including a large number of persons quite helpless, from old age, blindness, and other infirmities.

The scenes were much the same as we have described in connection with other places.

There is, however, one aspect of the harshness and cruelty practised on the Strathconon people, not applicable in many other cases, namely, that in most instances where they settled down and reclaimed land, they were afterwards re-evicted, and the lands brought into cultivation by themselves, taken from them, without any compensation whatever, and given at enhanced rents to large farmers.

This is specially true of those who settled down in the Black Isle, where they reclaimed a great deal of waste now making some of the best farms in that district.

The Strathconon evictions are worthy of note for the forcible illustration they furnish of how by these arbitrary and unexpected removals, hardships and ruin have frequently been brought upon families and communities who were at one time in contented and comfortable circumstances.

At one time, and previous to the earlier evictions, perhaps no glen of its size in the Highlands had a larger population than Strathconon.

The club farm system, once so common in the North, seems to have been peculiarly successful here. Hence a large proportion of the people were well to do, but when suddenly called upon to give up their hill pasture, and afterwards their arable land, the trials and difficulties of new con-

59

ditions had to be encountered.

As a rule, in most of these Highland evictions, the evicted were lost sight of, they having either emigrated to foreign lands or become absorbed in the ever-increasing population of the large towns.

In the case of Strathconon it was different, as has already been stated; many of the families evicted were allowed to settle on some of the wildest unreclaimed land in the Black Isle.

Their subsequent history there, and the excellent agricultural condition into which they in after years brought their small holdings, is a standing refutation of the charge so often made against the Highland people, that they are lazy and incapable of properly cultivating the land.

Respecting the estates of Drynie and Kilcoy on the BLACK ISLE, a correspondent, who says, "I well remember my excessive grief when my father had to leave the farm which his forefathers had farmed for five generations", writes:—

"All the tenants from the east of Drynie, as far as Craigiehow, were turned out, one by one, to make room for one large tenant, Mr Robertson, who had no less than four centres for stackyards.

A most prosperous tenantry were turned out to make room for him, and what is the end of it all!

Mr Robertson has come to grief as a farmer, and now holds a very humble position in the town of Inverness.

Drumderfit used to be occupied by fifteen or sixteen tenants who were gradually, and from time to time, evicted, during the last fifty years.

Balnakyle was tenanted by five very comfortable and respectable farmers, four of whom were turned out within the last thirty years; Balnaguie was occupied by three; Torr by six; and Croft-cruive by five; the once famous names of Drum-na-marg and Moreton are now extinct, as well as the old tenantry whose forefathers farmed these places for generations.

The present farm of Kilcoy includes a number of holdings whose tenants were evicted to make room for one large farmer;" and this is equally true of many others in the district.

Nothing can better illustrate the cruel manner in which the ancient tenantry of the country have been treated than these facts.

Why 229 islanders ended up destitute in Canada

No one was evicted from the ISLAND OF LEWIS, in the strict sense of the term, but 2231 souls had to leave it between 1851 and 1863.

To pay their passage money, their inland railway fares on arrival, and to provide them with clothing and other furnishings, the late Sir James Matheson paid a sum of £11,855.

Notwithstanding all this expenditure, many of these poor people would have died from starvation on their arrival without the good offices of friends in Canada.

In 1841, before Mr Matheson bought it, a cargo of emigrants from the Lews arrived at Quebec late in the autumn, accompanied by a Rev Mr Maclean, sent out to minister to their spiritual wants, but it appears that no provision had been made for the more pressing demands of a severe Canadian winter; and were it not for the Saint Andrew's Society of Montreal, every soul of them would have been starved to death that winter in a strange land.

The necessities of the case, and how this patriotic Society saved their countrymen from a horrid death will be seen on perusal of the following minutes, extracted from the books of the Society, during the writer's recent tour in Canada:— "A special meeting of the office-bearers was summoned on the 20th September, 1841, to take into consideration an application made by Mr Morris, President of the Emigration Association of the district of St Francis, for some pecuniary aid to a body of 229 destitute emigrants who had recently arrived from the Island of Lewis (Scotland), and who were then supported chiefly by the contributions of the charitable inhabitants of the town of Sherbrooke and its neighbourhood.

Mr Morris' letter intimated that unless other assistance was received, it would be impossible for these emigrants to outlive the winter, as they were in a state of utter destitution, and the inhabitants of the township could not support so large a number of persons from their own unaided resources.

The meeting decided that the Constitution of the Society prohibited them from applying its funds to an object like the one presented — it did not appear to authorise the granting of relief from its funds except to cases of destitution in the city; but as this case appeared of an urgent nature, and one particularly calling for assistance, Messrs Hew Ramsay and Neil M'Intosh were appointed to collect subscriptions on behalf of the emigrants.

This committee acquitted itself with great diligence and success, having collected the handsome sum of £234, the whole of which was, at different times, remitted to Mr Morris, and expended by him in this charity.

Letters were received from Mr Morris, expressing the gratitude of the emigrants for this large and timely aid, which was principally the means of keeping them from starvation". The whole of these emigrants are now in easy circumstances.

The idea of sending out a minister and nothing else, in such circumstances, makes one shudder to think of the uses which are sometimes made of the clergy, and how, in such cases, the Gospel they are supposed not only to preach but to practise, is only in many cases caricatured.

The provisions sent by the Society had to be forwarded to where these starving emigrants were, a distance of 80 miles from Sherbrooke, on sledges, through a trackless and dense forest.

The descendants of these people now form a happy and prosperous community at Lingwick and Winslow.

Deaf pauper woman's house demolished about her ears

LECKMELM, a small property, in the parish of Lochbroom, changed hands in 1879, Mr A C Pirie, paper manufacturer, Aberdeen, having purchased it for £19,000 from Colonel Davidson, now of Tulloch.

No sooner did it come into Mr Pirie's possession than a notice, dated 2nd November, 1879, in the following terms, was issued to all the tenants:—

"I am instructed by Mr Pirie, proprietor of Leckmelm, to give you notice that the present arrangements by which you hold the cottage, byre, and other buildings, together with lands on that estate, will cease from and after the term of Martinmas, 1880; and further, I am instructed to intimate to you that at the said term of Martinmas, 1880, Mr Pirie proposes taking the whole arable and pasture lands, but that he is desirous of making arrangements whereby you may continue tenant of the cottage upon terms and conditions yet to be settled upon.

I have further to inform you that unless you and the other tenants at once prevent your sheep and other stock from grazing or trespassing upon the enclosures and hill, and other lands now in the occupation or possession of the said Mr Pirie, he will not, upon any conditions, permit you to remain in the cottage you now occupy, after the said term of Martinmas, 1880, but will clear all off the estate, and take down the cottages".

This notice affected twenty-three families, numbering above one hundred souls. The stock allowed them was 72 head of cattle, 8 horses, and 320 sheep.

The arable portion of Leckmelm was about the best tilled and the most productive land in possession of any crofters in the parish.

The intention of the new proprietor was strictly carried out. At Martinmas, 1880, he took every inch of land — arable and pastoral — into his own hands, and thus by one cruel stroke, reduced a comfortable tenantry from comparative affluence and independence to the position of mere cottars and day labourers.

With the exception of one, all the tenants who remained are still permitted to live in their old cottages, but they are not permitted to keep a living thing about them — not even a hen.

They are existing in a state of abject dependence on Mr Pirie's will and that of his servants; and in a constant state of terror that they will even be turned out of their cottages.

In place of milk, butter and cheese in fair abundance they now have to be satisfied with sugar, treacle or whatever else they can buy, to eat with their porridge and potatoes. Their supply of meat, bred by themselves, is gone forever.

As regards work and the necessaries of life, they have been reduced to that of common navvies.

Two, a man and his wife, if not more, have since been provided for by the Parochial authorities, and, no doubt, that will ultimately be the fate of many more of this once thriving and contented people.

When the notices of removal were received, the Rev John MacMillan, Free Church minister of this parish, called public attention to Mr Pirie's proceedings in the Northern newspapers, and soon the eye of the whole country was directed to this modern evictor — a man, in other respects, reputed considerate and even kind to those under him in his business of paper manufacturing in Aberdeen.

People, in their simplicity, for years back, thought that evictions on such a large scale, in the face of a more enlightened public opinion, had become mere unpleasant recollections of a barbarous past; forgetting that the same laws which permitted the clearances of Sutherland and other portions of the Scottish Highlands during the first half of the century were still in force.

At the urgent request of many friends of the Highland crofters, resident in Inverness, Mr MacMillan agreed to lay the case of his evicted parishioners before the public.

Early in December, 1880, he delivered an address in Inverness to one of the largest and most enthusiastic meetings which has ever been held in that town.

Mr MacMillan after a few opening remarks giving a resumé of the purchase of the estate and subsequent instructions to tenants declared:-

"To strike terror into their hearts, first of all, two houses were pulled down, I might say about the ears of their respective occupants, without any warning whatever, except a verbal one of the shortest kind.

The first was a deaf pauper woman, about middle life, living alone for years in a bothy of her own, altogether apart from the other houses, beside a purling stream, where she had at all seasons pure water to drink even if her bread was at times somewhat scanty.

After this most cruel eviction no provision was made for the helpless woman, but she was allowed to get shelter elsewhere or anywhere, as best she could.

Mrs Campbell was a widow with two children; after the decease of her husband she tried to support herself and them by serving in gentlemen's families as a servant.

Her house also was pulled down about her ears. This

woman has since gone to America, the asylum of many an evicted family from hearth and home.

Such tragedies as I have mentioned roused some of us to remonstrate with the actors engaged in them, and to the best of our ability to expose their conduct, and, furthermore, we have brought them to the bar of public judgment to pass their verdict, which I hope before all is over, will be one of condemnation and condign punishment".

Later in the speech he said:— "But there is another way which depopulates our country ...

There are many proprietors who are inch by inch secretly and stealthily laying waste the country and undermining the well-being of our people.

I have some of these gentlemen before my mind at the moment. When they took possession of their estates all promised fair and well, but by-and-bye the fatal blow was struck, to dispossess the people of their sheep.

Mark that *first move* and resist it to the utmost.

As long as tenants have a hold of the hill pasture by sheep, and especially if it be what we term a commonage or club farm, it is impossible to lay it waste in part.

But once you snap this tie asunder, you are henceforth at the mercy of the owner to do with you as he pleases.

When a tenant dies, or removes otherwise, the order goes forth that his croft or lot is to be laid waste.

It is not given to a neighbouring tenant, except in some instances, nor to a stranger, to occupy it.

In this inch-by-inch clearance, the work of depopulation is effected in a few years, or in a generation at most, quite as effectually as by the more glaring and reprehensible method".

Describing the character of the Highlanders, as shown by their conduct in our Highland regiments, and the impossibility of recruiting from them in future, if harsh evictions are not stopped, the minister said that "about the year 1808 the stream of Highland soldiery, which had been gradually ebbing, gave symptoms of running completely dry.

Recruits for Highland regiments could not be obtained for the simple reason that the Highlands had been depopulated.

Six regiments which from the date of their foundation had worn the kilt and bonnet were ordered to lay aside their distinctive uniform and henceforth became merged into the ordinary line corps.

From the mainland the work of destruction passed rapidly to the isles.

These remote resting-places of the Celt were quickly cleared, during the first ten years of the great war, Skye had given 4000 of its sons to the army.

It has been computed that 1600 Skyemen stood in the ranks at Waterloo.

Today in Skye, as far as the eye can reach, nothing but a bare brown waste is to be seen, where still the mounds and ruined gables rise over the melancholy landscapes, sole vestiges of a soldier race for ever passed away".

'Petty tyranny was scarcely creditable'

In January, 1882, news had reached Inverness that Murdo Munro, one of the most comfortable tenants on the Leckmelm property, had been turned out, with his wife and young family, in the snow.

Munro was too independent for the local managers, and to some extent led the people in their opposition to Mr Pirie's proceedings: he was first persecuted and afterwards evicted in the most cruel fashion.

Other reasons were later given for the eviction but it has been shown conclusively, in a report published at the time, that these reasons were an after-thought.

Alexander MacKenzie entitled his report "The Leckmelm Evictions". At the time he was editor of the 'Celtic Magazine', a fellow of the Society of Antiquaries of Scotland and a Dean of Guild of Inverness.

An extract from it reads:—

"I have made the most careful and complete inquiry possible among Mr Pirie's servants, the tenants, and the people of Ullapool. Mr Pirie's local manager informed me that he never had any fault to find with Munro, that he always found him quite civil, and that he had nothing to say against him.

The tenants, without exception, spoke of him as a good neighbour. The people of Ullapool, without exception, so far as I could discover, after enquiries from the leading men in every section of the community, speak well of him, and condemn Mr Pirie.

Munro is universally spoken of as one of the best and most industrious workmen in the whole parish, and, by his industry and sobriety, he has been able to save a little money in Leckmelm, where he was able to keep a fairly good stock on his small farm, and worked steadily with a horse and cart.

The stock handed over by him to Mr Pirie consisted of 1 bull, 2 cows, 1 stirk, 1 Highland pony, and about 40 sheep, which represented a considerable saving.

Several of the other tenants had a similar stock, and some of them had even more, all of which they had to dispense with under the new arrangements, and consequently lost the annual income in money and produce available therefrom.

We all know that the sum received for this stock cannot last long, and cannot be advantageously invested in anything else.

The people must now live on their small capital, instead of what it produced, so long as it lasts, after which they are sure to be helpless, and many of them become chargeable to the parish.

The system of petty tyrany which prevails at Leckmelm is scarcely creditable.

Contractors have been told not to employ Munro. For this I have the authority of some of the contractors themselves.

Local employers of labour were requested not to employ any longer people who had gone to look on among the crowd, while Munro's family, goods, and furniture, were being turned out.

Letters were received by others complaining of the same thing from higher quarters, and threatening ulterior consequences.

During the eviction the mother and children wept piteously. Many of the neighbours, afraid to succour, or shelter them, were visibly affected to tears.

The whole scene was such that, if Mr Pirie could have

seen it, I feel sure that he would never consent to be held responsible for another.

His humanity would soon drive his stern ideas of legal right out of his head, and we would hear no more of evictions at Leckmelm".

Those of the tenants who are still at Leckmelm are permitted to remain in their cottages as half-yearly tenants but are liable to be removed at any moment that their absolute lord may take it into his head to evict them; or, what is much more precarious, when they may give the slightest offence to any of his meanest subordinates.

How many of the evicted found peace in Canada

GLENGARRY was peopled down to the end of last century with a fine race of men.

In 1745, six hundred followed the chief of Glengarry to the battle of Culloden.

But a few years later many emigrated to the United States in search of a better life. They felt the chief wasn't doing enough for them although they were in comfortable circumstances.

Notwithstanding this semi-voluntary exodus, Major John Macdonell of Lochgarry, was able in 1777, to raise a fine regiment — the 76th or Macdonald Highlanders — numbering 1086 men, 750 of whom were Highlanders mainly from the Glengarry property.

In 1794, Alexander Macdonnell of Glengarry, raised a Fencible regiment, described as "a handsome body of men", of whom one-half were enlisted on the same estate.

On being disbanded in 1802, these men were again so shabbily treated, that they followed the example of the men of the "Forty-five", and emigrated in a body, with their families, to Canada.

They afterwards distinguished themselves as part of the "Glengarry Fencibles" of Canada, in defence of their adopted country, and called their settlement there after their native glen in Scotland.

The chiefs of Glengarry drove away their people, only, as in most other cases of the Highlands, to be ousted soon afterwards themselves.

The Glengarry property at one time covered an area of nearly 200 square miles, and to-day, while many of their expatriated vassals are landed proprietors and in affluent circumstances in Canada, not an inch of the old possessions of the ancient and powerful family of Glengarry remains to the descendants of those who caused the banishment of a poeple who, on many a well-fought field, shed their blood for their chief and country.

In 1853, every inch of the ancient heritage was possessed by the stranger, except Knoydart in the west, and this has long ago become the property of one of the Bairds.

In the year named, young Glengarry was a minor, his mother, the widow of the late chief, being one of his trustees.

She does not appear to have learned any lesson of wisdom from the past misfortunes of her house.

Indeed, considering her limited power and possessions, she was comparatively the worst of them all.

The tenants of Knoydart, like all other Highlanders, had suffered severely during and after the potato famine in 1846 and 1847, and some of them got into arrears with a year and some with two years' rent, but they were fast clearing it off.

Mrs Macdonell and her factor determined to evict every crofter on her property, to make room for sheep.

In the spring of 1853, they were all served with summonses of removal, accompanied by a message that Sir John Macneil, chairman of the Board of Supervision, had agreed to convey them to Australia.

Their feelings were not considered worthy of the slightest consideration.

They were not even asked whether they would prefer to follow their countrymen to America and Canada.

The people, however, had no alternative but to accept any offer made to them. They could not get an inch of land on any of the neighbouring estates, and any one who would give them a night's shelter was threatened with eviction.

It was afterwards found not convenient to transport them to Australia, and it was then intimated to the poor creatures, as if they were nothing but common slaves to be disposed of at will, that they would be taken to North America, and that a ship would be at Isle Ornsay, in the Isle of Skye, in a few days, to receive them, and that they *must* go on board.

The *Sillery* soon arrived. Mrs Macdonell and her factor came all the way from Edinburgh to see the people hounded across in boats, and put on board this ship whether they wanted to not.

An eye-witness who described the proceeding at the time, in a now rare pamphlet, and whom we met a few years ago in Nova Scotia, characterises the scene as heart-rending.

"The wail of the poor women and children as they were torn away from their homes would háve melted a heart of stone".

Some few families, principally cottars, refused to go, in spite of every influence brought to bear upon them; and the treatment they afterwards received was cruel beyond belief.

The houses, not only of those who went, but of those who remained, were burnt and levelled to the ground.

The Strath was dotted all over with black spots, showing where yesterday stood the habitations of men.

The scarred half-burned wood — couples, rafters, cabars — were strewn about in every direction.

Stooks of corn and plots of unlifted potatoes could be seen on all sides, but man was gone.

No voice could be heard.

Those who refused to go aboard the *Sillery* were in hiding among the rocks and the caves, while their friends were packed off like so many African slaves to the Cuban market.

No mercy was shown to those who refused to emigrate; their few articles of furniture were thrown out of their houses after them — beds, chairs, tables, pots, stoneware, clothing, in many cases, rolling down the hill.

What took years to erect and collect were destroyed and scattered in a few minutes.

"From house to house, from hut to hut, and from barn to barn, the factor and his menials proceeded, carrying on the work of demolition, until there was scarcely a human habitation left standing in the district.

Able-bodied men who, if the matter would rest with a mere trial of physical force, would have bound the factor and his party hand and foot, stood aside as dumb spectators.

Women wrung their hands and cried aloud, children ran to and fro dreadfully frightened; and while all this work of demolition and destruction was going on no opposition was offered by the inhabitants, no hand was lifted, no stone cast, no angry word was spoken".

The few huts left undemolished were occupied by the paupers, but before the factor left for the south even they were warned not to give any shelter to the evicted, or their huts would assuredly meet with the same fate.

Eleven families, numbering in all over sixty persons, mostly old and decrepit men and women, and helpless children, were exposed that night, and many of them long afterwards, to the cold air, without shelter of any description beyond what little they were able to save out of the wreck of their burnt dwellings.

We feel unwilling to inflict pain on the reader by the recitation of the untold cruelties perpetrated on the poor Highlanders of Knoydart, but doing so may, perhaps, serve a good purpose.

It may convince the evil-doer that his work shall not be forgotten, and any who may be disposed to follow the example of past evictors may hesitate before they proceed to immortalise themselves in such a hateful manner.

We shall, therefore, quote a few cases from the pamphlet already referred to:—

John Macdugald, aged about 50, with a wife and family, was a cottar, and earned his subsistence chiefly by fishing.

He was in bad health, and had two of his sons in the hospital, at Elgin, ill of smallpox, when the *Sillery* was sent to convey the Knoydart people to Canada.

He refused to go on that occasion owing to the state of his health, and his boys being at a distance under medical treatment.

The factor and the officers, however, arrived, turned Macdugald and his family adrift, put their bits of furniture out on the field, and in a few minutes levelled their house to the ground.

The whole family had now no shelter but the broad canopy of heaven.

The mother and the youngest of the children could not sleep owing to the cold, and the father, on account of his sickness, kept wandering about all night near where his helpless family lay down to repose.

After the factor and the officers left the district Macdugald and his wife went back to the ruins of their house, collected some of the stones and turf into something like walls, threw a few cabars across, covered them over with blankets, old sails, and turf, and then, with their children, crept underneath, trusting that they would be allowed, at least for a time, to take shelter under this temporary covering.

But, alas! they were doomed to bitter disappointment.

A week had not elapsed when the local manager, accompanied by a *posse* of officers and menials, traversed the country and levelled to the ground every hut or shelter erected by the evicted peasantry.

Macdugald was at this time away from Knoydart; his wife was at Inverie, distant about six miles, seeing a sick relatve; the oldest children were working at the shore; and in the hut, when the manager came with the "levellers", he found none of the family except Lucy and Jane, the two youngest.

The moment they saw the officers they screamed and fled for their lives.

The demolition of the shelter was easily accomplished — it was but the work of two or three minutes; and, this over, the officers and menials of the manager amused themselves by seizing hold of chairs, stools, tables, spinning-wheels, or any other light articles, and throwing them a considerable distance from the hut.

Even chapel ruin was no sanctuary for MacKinnons

John Mackinnon, a cottar, aged 44, with a wife and six children, had his house pulled down. They had no place to put their heads for the first night or two, so had to burrow among the rocks near the shore!

When he thought that the factor and his party had left the district, he emerged from the rocks, surveyed the ruins of his former dwelling, saw his furniture and other effects exposed to the elements, and now scarcely worth the lifting.

The demolition was so complete that he considered it

utterly impossible to make any use of the ruins of his old house.

The ruins of an old chapel, however, were near at hand, and parts of the walls were still standing; thither Mackinnon proceeded with his family, and having swept away some rubbish and removed some grass and nettles, they placed a few cabars up to one of the walls, spread some sails and blankets across, brought in some meadow hay, and laid it in a corner for a bed, stuck a piece of iron into the wall in another corner, on which they placed a crook, then kindled a fire to cook food.

Mackinnon is a tall man, but poor and unhealthy-looking.

His wife is a poor weak woman, evidently struggling with a diseased constitution and dreadful trials.

The boys, Ronald and Archibald, were lying in a "bed" — (may I call a "pickle" hay on the bare ground a bed?) — suffering from rheumatism and colic.

The other children are apparently healthy enough as yet, but very ragged.

There is no door to their wretched abode, consequently every breeze and gust that blow have free ingress to the inmates.

Mackinnon's wife was pregnant when she was turned out of her house among the rocks.

In about four days after she had a premature birth; and this and her exposure to the elements, and the want of proper shelter and nutritious diet, has brought on consumption from which there is no chance whatever of her recovery.

There was something very solemn indeed in this scene. Here, amid the ruins of the old sanctuary, where the ivy tried to screen the grey moss-covered stones, where nettles and grass grew up, where the floor was damp, where there were no doors nor windows, nor roof, a Christian family was obliged to take shelter!

One would think that as Mackinnon took refuge amid the ruins of this most singular place, that he would be let alone, that he would not any longer be molested by man.

But alas! that was not to be.

The manager of Knoydart and his minions appeared, and invaded this helpless family, even within the walls of the sanctuary.

They pulled down the sticks and sails he set up within its ruins — put his wife and children out on the cold shore — threw his tables, stools, chairs, etc., over the walls — burnt up the hay on which they slept — put out the fire, and then left the district.

Four times have these officers broken in upon poor Mackinnon in this way, destroying his place of shelter, and sent him and his family adrift on the cold coast of Knoydart.

Another case involved Elizabth Gillies, a widow, aged 60 years. This is a most lamentable case.

Neither age, sex, nor circumstance saved this poor creature from the most wanton and cruel aggression.

Her house was on the brow of a hill, near a stream that formed the boundary between a large sheep farm and the land of the tenants of Knoydart.

Widow Gillies was warned to quit like the rest of the tenants, and was offered a passage first to Australia and then to Canada, but she refused to go, saying she could do nothing in Canada.

The widow, however, made no promises, and the factor went away.

She had then a nice young daughter staying with her, but ere the vessel that was to convey the Knoydart people arrived at Isle Ornsay, this young girl died, and poor Widow Gillies was left alone.

When the time for pulling down the houses arrived, it was hoped that some mercy would have been shown to this poor, bereaved widow, but there was none.

Widow Gillies was sitting inside her house when the factor and officers arrived.

They ordered her to remove herself and her effects instantly, as they were, they said, to pull down the house!

She asked them where she would remove to; the factor would give no answer, but continued insisting on her leaving the house.

She refused.

Two men then took hold of her, and tried to pull her out by force, but she sat down beside the fire, and would not move an inch.

One of the assistants threw water on the fire and extinguished it, and then joined the other two in forcibly removing the poor widow from the house.

At first she struggled hard, seized hold of every post or stone within her reach, taking a death grasp of each to keep possession.

But the officers were too many and too cruel for her.

They struck her over the fingers, and compelled her to let go her hold, and then all she could do was greet and cry out murder!

She was ultimately thrust out at the door, from where she crept on her hands and feet to a dyke side, being quite exhausted and panting for breath, owing to her hard struggle with three powerful men.

Whenever they got her outside, the work of destruction immediately commenced.

Stools, chairs, tables, cupboard, spinning-wheel, bed, blankets, straw, dishes, pots, and chest, were thrown out in the gutter.

They broke down the partitions, took down the crook from over the fire-place, destroyed the hen roosts, and then beat the hens out through the broad vent in the roof of the house.

This done, they set to work on the walls outside with picks and iron levers.

They pulled down the thatch, cut the couples, and in a few minutes the walls fell out, while the roof fell in with a dismal crash!

When the factor and his party were done with this house, they proceeded to another district, pulling down and destroying dwelling-places as they went along.

The shades of night at last closed in, and here was the poor helpless widow sitting like a pelican, alone and cheerless.

Allan Macdonald, a cottar, whose house was also pulled down, ran across the hill to see how the poor widow had been treated, and found her moaning beside the dyke.

He led her to where his own children had taken shelter, treated her kindly, and did all he could to comfort her under the circumstances.

Another case is that of Archibald Macisaac, crofter, aged 66, with a 54-year-old wife and a family of ten children.

Archibald's house, byre, barn, and stable were levelled to the ground.

The furniture of the house was thrown down the hill, and a general destruction then commenced.

The roof, fixtures, and woodwork were smashed to pieces, the walls razed to the very foundation, and all that was left for poor Archibald to look upon was a black dismal wreck.

Twelve human beings were thus deprived of their home in less than half-an-hour.

It was grossly illegal to have destroyed the barn, for, according even to the law of Scotland, the outgoing or removing tenant is entitled to the use of the barn until his crops are disposed of.

His wife and children wept, but the old man said, "Neither weeping nor reflection will now avail; we must prepare some shelter".

The children collected some cabars and turf, and in the hollow between two ditches, the old man constructed a rude shelter for the night, and having kindled a fire and gathered in his family, they all engaged in family worship and sung psalms as usual.

Next morning they examined the ruins, picked up some broken pieces of furniture, dishes, etc., and then made another addition to their shelter in the ditch.

Matters went on this way for about a week, when the local manager and his men came down upon them, and after much abuse for daring to take shelters on the lands of Knoydart, they destroyed the shelter and put old Archy and his people out on the hill again.

I found Archibald and his numerous family still at Knoydart and in a shelter beside the old ditch.

Any residence more wretched I have never witnessed.

A feal, or turf erection, about 3 feet high, 4 feet broad, and about 5 feet long, was at the end of the shelter, and this formed the sleeping place of the mother and her five daughters!

They creep in and out on their knees, and their bed is just a layer of hay on the cold earth of the ditch. There is surely monstrous cruelty in this treatment of British females, and can we not perceive a monstrous injustice in treating them worse than slaves because they refuse to allow themselves to be packed off to the Colonies just like so many bales of manufactured goods?

Again:—

Donald Maceachan, a cottar at Arar, married, with a wife, and five children.

This poor man, his wife, and children were fully twenty-three nights without any shelter but the broad and blue heavens.

They kindled a fire, and prepared their food beside a rock, and then slept in the open air.

Just imagine the condition of this poor mother, Donald's wife, nursing a delicate child, and subjected to merciless storms of wind and rain during a long October night.

One of these melancholy nights the blankets that

covered them were frozen and white with frost.

Alexander Macdonald, aged 40 years, with a wife and family of four children, had his house pulled down.

His wife was pregnant; still the levellers thrust her out, and then put the children out after her.

The husband argued, remonstrated, and protested, but it was all in vain; for in a few minutes all he had for his home was a lot of rubbish, blackened rafters, and heaps of stones.

The levellers laughed at him and at his protests, and when their work was over, moved away, leaving him to find refuge the best way he could.

Alexander had, like the rest of his evicted brethren, to burrow among the rocks and in caves until he put up a temporary shelter amid the wreck of his old habitation, but from which he was repeatedly driven away.

For three days Alexander Macdonald's wife lay sick beside a bush, where, owing to terror and exposure to cold, she had a miscarriage.

She was then moved to the shelter of the walls of her former house, and for three days she lay so ill that her life was despaired of.

Sick woman forced from bed and left at ditch for seven hours

Catherine Mackinnon, aged about 50 years, unmarried; Peggy Mackinnon, aged about 48 years, unmarried; and Catherine Macphee (a half-sister of the two Mackinnons), also unmarried; occupied one house.

Catherine Mackinnon was for a long time sick, and she was confined to bed when the factor and his party came to beat down the house.

At first they requested her to get up and walk out, but her sisters said she could not, as she was so unwell.

They answered, "Oh, she is scheming"; the sisters said

she was not, that she had been ill for a considerable time, and the sick woman herself, who then feebly spoke, said she was quite unfit to be removed, but if God spared her and bestowed upon her better health that she would remove of her own accord.

This would not suffice; *they forced her out of bed, sick as she was, and left her beside a ditch from 10.00am to 5pm,* when, afraid that she would die, as she was seriously unwell, they removed her to a house, and provided her with cordials and warm clothing.

Peggy and her half-sister Macphee are still burrowing among the ruins of their old home. When I left Knoydart last week there were no hopes whatever of Catherine Mackinnon's recovery.

Retribution has overtaken the evictors, and is it a wonder that the chiefs of Glengarry are now as little known, and own as little of their ancient domains in the Highlands as their devoted clansmen?

There is now scarcely one of the name of Macdonald in the wide district once inhabited by thousands.

It is a huge wilderness in which barely anything is met but wild animals and sheep, and the few keepers and shepherds necessary to take care of them.

In three years 5390 souls were driven from the glens

A chief's widow, *Marsali Bhinneach* — Marjory, daughter of Sir Ludovick Grant of Dalvey, widow of Duncan Macdonnell of Glengarry, who died in 1788 — gave the whole of Glencruaich as a sheep farm to one south country shepherd, and to make room for him she evicted over 500 people from their ancient homes.

The bad example of this heartless woman was unfortunately imitated afterwards by her daughter Elizabeth, who, in 1801, cleared Strathglass almost to a man of its inhabitants.

No less than 799 took ship at Fort William and Isle Martin from Strathglass, the Aird, Glen Urquhart, and the neighbouring districts, all for Pictou, Nova Scotia; while in the following year, 473 from the same district left Fort William, for Upper Canada, and 128 for Pictou.

Five hundred and fifty went aboard another ship at Knoydart, many of whom were from Strathglass.

In 1803, four different batches of 120 souls each, by four different ships, left Strathglass, also for Pictou; while not a few went away with emigrants from other parts of the Highlands.

During these three years we find that no less than 5390 were driven out of these Highland glens, and it will be seen that a very large proportion of them were evicted from Strathglass by the daughter of the notorious *Marsali Bhinneach.*

From among the living cargo of one of the vessels which sailed from Fort William no less than fifty-three souls died, on the way out, of an epidemic; and, on the arrival of the living portion of the cargo at Pictou, they were shut in on a narrow point of land, from whence they were not allowed to communicate with any of their friends who had gone before them, for fear of communicating the contagion. Here they suffered indescribable hardships.

Cruel truth of summons to inn

In 1830 every man who held la d on the property was requested to meet his chief at the local inn of Cannich.

They all obeyed, and were there at the appointed time, but no chief came to meet them.

The factor soon turned up, however, and informed them that the laird had decided not to enter into negotiation or any new arrangements with them that day.

They were all in good circumstances, without any arrears of rent, but were practically banished from their homes in the most inconsiderate and cruel manner, and it afterwards became known that their farms had been secretly let to sheep farmers from the south, without the knowledge of the native population in possession.

Mr Colin Chisholm, who was present at the meeting at

Cannich, writes:— "I leave you to imagine the bitter grief and disappointment of men who attended with glowing hopes in the morning, but had to tell their families and dependents in the evening that they could see no alternative before them but the emigrant ship.

It did not, however, come to that. The late Lord Lovat, hearing of the harsh proceedings, proposed to one of the large sheep farmers on his neighbouring property to give up his farm, his lordship offering to give full value for the stock, so that he might divide it amongst those evicted from the Chisholm estate.

This arrangement was amicably carried through, and at the next Whitsunday — 1831 — the evicted tenants from Strathglass came into possession of the large sheep farm of Glenstrathfarrar, and paid over to the late tenant of the farm every farthing of the value set upon the stock by two of the leading valuators in the country; a fact which conclusively proved that the Strathglass tenants were quite capable of holding their own, and perfectly able to meet all claims that could be made upon them by their old proprietor and unnatural chief.

They became very comfortable in their new homes; but about fifteen years after their eviction from Strathglass they were again removed to make room for deer.

On this occasion the late Lord Lovat gave them similar holdings on other portions of his property, and the sons and grandsons of the evicted tenants of Strathglass are now, on the Lovat property, among the most respectable and comfortable middle-class farmers in the county.

The result of the Strathglass evictions was that only two of the ancient native stock remained in possession of an inch of land on the estate of Chisholm.

When the present Chisholm came into possession he found, on his return from Canada, only that small remnant of his own name and clan to receive him.

He brought back a few Chisholms from the Lovat property, and re-established on his old farm a tenant who had been evicted nineteen years before from the holding in which his father and grandfather died.

The great-grandfather was killed at Culloden, having been shot while carrying his commander, young Chisholm, mortally wounded, from the field.

The gratitude of that chief's successors had been shown by his ruthless eviction from the ancient home of his ancestors; but it is gratifying to find the present chief making some reparation by bringing back and liberally supporting the representatives of such a devoted follower of his forbears.

The present Chisholm, who has the character of being a good landlord, is descended from a distant collateral branch of the family.

The evicting Chisholms, and their offspring have, however, every one of them, disappeared, and Mr Colin Chisholm informs us that there is not a human being now in Strathglass of the descendants of the chief, or of the south country farmers, who were the chief instruments in evicting the native population.

To give the reader an idea of the class of men who occupied this district, it may be stated that of the descendants of those who lived in Glen Canaich, one of the smaller glens, at one time thickly populated in the Strath, but now a perfect wilderness — there lived in the present generation, no less than three colonels, one major, three captains, three lieutenants, seven ensigns, one bishop, and fifteen priests.

How 15 farmers vanished ...

The modern clearances which took place within the last quarter of a century in Guisachan, Strathglass, by Sir Dudley Marjoribanks, were described in all their phases before a Committee of the House of Commons in 1872.

The Inspector of Poor for the parish of Kiltarlity wrote a letter which was brought before the Committee, with a statement from another source that, "in 1855, there were 16 farmers on the estate; the number of cows they had was 62, and horses, 24; the principal farmer had 2000 sheep, the next 1000, and the rest between them 1200, giving a total of 4200.

Now (1873) there is but one farmer, and he leaves at Whitsunday; all these farmers lost the holdings on which they ever lived in competency; indeed, it is well known that some of them were able to lay by some money.

They have been sent to the four quarters of the globe, or to vegetate in Sir Dudley's dandy cottages at Tomich, made more for show than convenience, where they have to depend on his employment or charity.

To prove that all this is true, take at random, the smith, the shoemaker, or the tailor, and say whether the poverty and starvation were then or now?

For instance, under the old *régime*, the smith farmed a piece of land which supplied the wants of his family with meal and potatoes; he had two cows, a horse, and a score or two of sheep on the hill; he paid £7 of yearly rent; he now has nothing but the bare walls of his cottage and smithy, for which he pays £10.

Of course he had his trade then as he has now.

Will he live more comfortably now than he did then?"

It was stated, at the same time, that, when Sir Dudley Marjoribanks bought the property, there was a population of 255 souls upon it, and Sir Dudley, in his examination, though he threw some doubt upon that statement, was quite unable to refute it.

The proprietor, on being asked, said that he did not evict any of the people.

But his questioner having said, "Then the tenants went away of their own free will", Sir Dudley replied, "I must not say so quite. I told them that when they had found other places to go to, I wished to have their farms".

They were, in point of fact, evicted as much as any others of the ancient tenantry of the Highlands, though it is but fair to say that the same harsh cruelty was not applied in their case as in many of the others recorded in these pages.

Paid to get out of Scotland!

In 1849 more than 500 souls in GLENELG petitioned the proprietor , Mr Baillie of Dochfour, to provide means of existence for them, by land reclamation and improvements. If this couldn't be done they asked for £3000 to finance an emigration programme.

Baillie accepted the latter proposal but gave only £2000. A further £500 came from the Highland Destitution Committee.

The money was needed for passage, free rations, a month's sustenance after the arrival of the party in Canada and some clothing for the more destitute.

Baillie was generous but, considering the suitability of the beautiful valley of Glenelg for arable and food-producing purposes, it is to be regretted that he did not decide upon utilizing the labour of the natives in bringing the district into a state of cultivation, rather than have paid so much to banish them to a foreign land.

That they would themselves have preferred this is beyond question.

Mr Mulock, father of the author of "John Halifax, Gentleman", an Englishman who could not be charged with any preconceived prejudices or partiality for the Highlanders, travelled at this period through the whole North, and ultimately published an account of what he had seen.

Regarding the Glenelg business, he says, as to their willingness to emigrate:— "To suppose that numerous families would as a matter of choice sever themselves from their loved soil and abolish all the associations of local and patriotic sentiment is an hypothesis too unnatural to be encouraged by any sober, well-regulated mind".

To satisfy himself, he called forty to fifty heads of families together at Glenelg, who had signed an agreement to emigrate, but who did not find room in the *Liscard*, and were left behind, after selling off everything they possessed, and were consequently reduced to a state of starvation.

"I asked", he says, "these poor creatures if, notwithstanding all their hardships, they were willing emigrants from their native land.

With one voice they assured me that nothing short of the impossibility of obtaining land or employment at home could drive them to seek the doubtful benefits of a foreign shore.

So far from the emigration being, at Glenelg, or Lochalsh, or South Uist, a spontaneous movement springing out of the wishes of the tenantry, I aver it to be, on the contrary, the product of desperation, the calamitous light of hopeless oppression visiting their sad hearts".

We have no hesitation in saying that this is not only true of those to whom Mr Mulock specially refers, but to almost every soul who has left the Highlands for the last sixty years.

Only those who know the people intimately, and the means adopted by factors, clergy, and others to produce an appearance of spontaneity on the part of the helpless tenantry, can understand the extent to which this statement is true.

If a judicious system had been applied of cultivating excellent land, capable of producing food in abundance, in Glenelg, there was not another property in the Highlands on which it was less necessary to send the people away than in that beautiful and fertile valley.

*   *   *   *   *   *   *   *   *

Great numbers were evicted from the Cameron country of Lochaber, especially from GLENDESSERAY and LOCHARKAIG side.

Indeed it is said that there were so few Camerons left in the district, that not a single tenant of the name attended the banquet given by the tenantry when the late Lochiel came into possession.

The details of Cameron evictions would be found pretty much the same as those in other places, except that an attempt has been made in this case to hold the factor entirely and solely responsible for the removal of this noble people, so renowned in the martial history of this country.

That is a question, however, which it is no part of our present purpose to discuss.

What we wish to expose is the unrighteous system which allowed such cruel proceedings to take place here and elsewhere, by landlord or factor.

When sheep skins became mightier than the sword!

The people of SKYE and the UIST, where the Macdonalds for centuries ruled in the manner of princes over a loyal and devoted people, were treated not a whit better than those on the mainland, when their services were no longer required to fight the battles of the Lords of the Isles, or to secure them their possessions, their dignity, and power.

Bha latha eile ann! There was another day!

When possessions were held by the sword, those who wielded them were highly valued, and well cared for.

Now that sheep skins are found sufficient, what could be more appropriate in the opinion of some of the sheepish chiefs of modern times than to displace the people who anciently secured and held the lands for real chiefs worthy of the name, and replace them by the animals that produced the modern sheep skins by which they hold their lands; especially when these were found to be better titles than the old ones — the blood and sinew of their ancient vassals.

Prior to 1849, the manufacture of kelp in the Outer Hebrides had been for many years a large source of income to the proprietors of those islands, and a considerable revenue to the inhabitants; the lairds, in consequence, for many years encouraged the people to remain, and it is alleged that they multiplied to a degree quite out of proportion to the means of subsistence within reach when kelp manufacture failed.

To make matters worse for the poor tenants, the rents were meanwhile raised by the proprietors to more than double — not because the land was considered worth more by itself, but because the possession of it enabled poor tenants to earn a certain sum a year from kelp made out of the seaware to which their holdings entitled them, and out of which the proprietor pocketed a profit of from £3 to £4 a ton, in addition to the enhanced rent obtained from the crofter for the land.

In these circumstances one would have thought that some consideration would have been shown to the people, who, it may perhaps be admitted, were found in the altered circumstances too numerous to obtain a livelihood in those islands; but such consideration does not appear to have been given — indeed the very reverse.

*   *   *   *   *   *   *   *

In 1849 Lord Macdonald decided to evict between 600 and 700 persons from Sollas, in North Uist, of which he was then proprietor.

They were at that time in a state of great misery from the failure of the potato crop.

Families had to live for weeks solely on shell-fish picked up on the sea-shore.

Some of the men were employed on drainage works, for which public money was advanced to the proprietors; but here, as in most other places throughout the Highlands, the money earned was applied by the factors to wipe off old arrears, while the people were permitted generally to starve.

His lordship having decided that they must go, notices of ejectment were served upon them, to take effect on the 15th of May, 1849.

They asked for delay to enable them to dispose of their effects to the best advantage at the summer markets. The plea was ignored. They were turned out of their houses, the doors locked and everything they possessed — cattle, crops, and peats — seized.

Even their bits of furniture were thrown out of doors in the manner which had long become fashion in such cases.

The season was too far advanced — towards the end of July — to start for Canada.

Before they could arrive there, the cold winter would be upon them, without means or money to provide against it.

They naturally rebelled, and the principal Sheriff-Substitute, Colquhoun, with his officers and a strong body of police left Inverness for North Uist, to eject them from their homes.

Naturally unwilling to proceed to extremes, on the arrival of the steamer at Armadale, they sent a messenger ashore to ask for instructions to guide them in case of resistance, or if possible to obtain a modification of his lordship's views.

Lord Macdonald had no instructions to give, but referred the Sheriff to Mr Cooper, his factor, whose answer was that the whole population of Sollas would be subject to eviction if they did not at once agree to emigrate.

A few men were arrested who obstructed the evictors on a previous occasion.

They were marched off to Lochmaddy by the police.

The work of destruction soon commenced.

At first no opposition was made by the poor people.

An eye-witness, whose sympathies were believed to be favourable to the proprietor, described some of the proceedings as follows:—

"In evicting Macpherson, the first case taken up, no opposition to the law officers was made. In two or three minutes the few articles of furniture he possessed — a bench, a chair, a broken chair, a barrel, a bag of wool, and two or three small articles, which comprised his whole household of goods and gear — were turned out of the door and his bothy left roofless.

The wife of the prisoner Macphail (one of those taken to Lochmaddy on the previous day) was the next evicted.

Her domestic plenishing was of the simplest character — its greatest and by far its most valuable part, being three small children, dressed in nothing more than a single coat of coarse blanketing, who played about her knee, while the poor woman, herself half clothed, with her face bathed in tears, and holding an infant in her arms, assured the Sheriff that she and her children were totally destitute and without food of any kind.

The Sheriff at once sent for the Inspector of the Poor, and ordered him to place the woman and her family on the poor's roll".

The next house was occupied by very old and infirm people, whom the Sheriff positively refused to evict.

He also refused to eject eight other families where an irregularity was discovered by him in the notices served upon them.

The next family ejected led to the almost solitary instance hitherto in the history of Highland evictions where the people made anything like real resistance.

This man was a crofter and a weaver, having a wife and nine children to provide for.

At this stage a crowd of men and women gathered on an eminence a little distance from the house, and gave the first indications of a hostile intention by raising shouts, as the police advanced to help in the work of demolition, accompanied by about a dozen men who came to their assistance in unroofing the houses from the other end of the island.

The crowd, exasperated at the conduct of their own neighbours, threw some stones at the latter. The police were then drawn up in two lines.

The furniture was thrown outside, the web was cut from the loom, and the terrified woman rushed to the door with an infant in her arms, exclaiming in a passionate and wailing voice — "Tha mo chlann air a bhi' air a muirt" (My children are to be murdered).

The crowd became excited, stones were thrown at the officers, their assistants were driven from the roof of the house, and they had to retire behind the police for shelter.

Volleys of stones and other missiles followed.

The police charged in two divisions.

There were some cuts and bruises on both sides.

The demolition was then allowed to go on without further opposition from the crowd.

Several heart-rending scenes followed, but we shall only give a description of the last which took place on that occasion, and which brought about a little delay in the cruel work.

In one case it was found necessary to remove the women out of the house by force.

"One of them threw herself upon the ground and fell into hysterics, uttering the most doleful sounds, and barking and yelling like a dog for about ten minutes.

Another, with many tears, sobs, and groans put up a petition to the Sheriff that they would leave the roof over part of her house, where she had a loom with cloth in it, which she was weaving; and a third woman, the eldest of the family, made an attack with a stick on an officer, and, missing him, she sprang upon him, and knocked off his hat.

So violently did this old woman conduct herself that two stout policemen had great difficulty in carrying her outside the door.

The excitement was again getting so strong that the factor agreed to allow them to occupy their houses until next spring, if the heads of familes signed an agreement to emigrate any time next year, from the 1st of February to the end of June.

Some agreed to these conditions, but the majority declined; and, in the circumstances, the people were permitted to go back to their unroofed and ruined homes for a few months longer.

Their cattle were, however, mostly taken possession of, and applied to the reduction of old arrears".

Four of the men were afterwards charged with deforcing the officers, and sentenced at Inverness Court of Justiciary each to four months' imprisonment.

The following year the district was completely and mercilessly cleared of all its remaining inhabitants, numbering 603 souls.

The Sollas evictions did not satisfy the evicting craze which his lordship afterwards so bitterly regretted. In 1851-53 he, or rather his trustee, determined to evict the people from all the villages.

Many died from deadly fever on emigrant ship

His lordship's position in regard to the proceedings was most unfortunate.

Donald Ross, writing as an eye-witness of these evictions, says —

"Some years ago Lord Macdonald incurred debts on his property to the extent of £200,000 sterling, and his lands being entailed, his creditors could not dispose of them, but they placed a trustee over them in order to intercept certain portions of the rent in payment of the debt.

Lord Macdonald, of course, continues to have an interest and a surveillance over the property in the matter of removals, the letting of the fishings and shootings, and the general improvement of his estates.

The trustee and the local factor under him have no particular interest in the property. nor in the people thereon, beyond collecting their quota of the rents for the creditors; consequently the property is mismanaged, and the crofter and cottar population are greatly neglected.

The tenants of SUISINISH and BORERAIG were the descendants of a long line of peasantry on the Macdonald estates, and were remarkable for their patience, loyalty, and general good conduct".

The only plea made at the time of evicting them was that of over-population.

Ten families received the usual summonses, and passages were secured for them in the *Hercules*, an unfortunate ship which sailed with a cargo of passengers under the auspices of a body calling itself "The Highland and Island Emigration Society .

A deadly fever broke out among the passengers, the ship was detained at Cork in consequence, and a large number of the passengers died of the epidemic.

After the sad fate of so many of those previously cleared out, in the ill-fated ship, it was generally thought that some compassion would be shown for those who had been still permitted to remain.

Not so, however. On the 4th of April 1853, they were all warned out of their holdings.

They petitioned and pleaded with his lordship to no purpose.

They were ordered to remove their cattle from the pasture, and themselves from their houses and lands.

Subsequently, however, they were informed that they would get land on another part of the estate — portions of a barren moor, quite unfit for cultivation.

In the middle of September following, Lord Macdonald's ground officer, with a body of constables, arrived, and at once proceeded to eject in the most heartless manner the whole population, numbering 32 families, and that at a period when the able-bodied male members of the families were away from home trying to earn something by which to pay their rents, and help to carry their families through the coming winter.

In spite of the wailing of the helpless women and children, the cruel work was proceeded with as rapidly as possible, and without the slightest apparent compunction.

The aged and infirm, some of them so frail that they could not move, were pushed and carried out.

"The scene was truly heart-rending. The women and children went about tearing their hair, and rending the heavens with their cries.

Mothers with tender infants at the breast looked helplessly on, while their effects and their aged and infirm relatives, were cast out, and the doors of their houses locked in their faces".

The young children, poor, helpless, little creatures, gathered in groups, and gave vent to their feelings in loud and bitter wailings.

"No mercy was shown to age or sex, all were indiscriminately thrust out and left to perish on the hills."

Untold cruelties were perpetrated on this occasion to the helpless creatures during the absence of their husbands and other principal breadwinners.

Donald Ross in his pamphlet, "Real Scottish Grievances", published in 1854, and who not only was an eye-witness, but generously supplied the people with a great quantity of food and clothing, describes several of the cases. I can only find room here, however, for his first.

Flora Robertson or Matheson, a widow, aged 96 years, was then residing with her son, Alexander Matheson, who had a small lot of land in Suisinish.

Her son was a widower, with four children; and shortly

before the time for evicting the people arrived, he went to labour at harvest in the south, taking his oldest boy with him.

The grandmother and the three other children were left in the house.

"When the evicting officers and factor arrived, the poor old woman was sitting on a couch outside the house.

The day being fine, her grandchildren lifted her out of bed and brought her to the door.

She was very frail; and it would have gladdened any heart to see how the two youngest of her grandchildren helped her along; how they seated her where there was most shelter; and then, how they brought her some clothing and clad her, and endeavoured to make her comfortable.

The gratitude of the old woman was unbounded in these little acts of kindness and compassion; and the poor children, on the other hand, felt highly pleased at finding their services so well appreciated.

Nothing could exceed the beauty of the scene. The sea was glittering with millions of little waves and globules, and looked like a lake of silver, gently agitated.

The hills, with the heather in full bloom, and with the wild flowers in their beauty, had assumed all the colours of the rainbow, and were most pleasant to the eye to look upon.

The crops of corn in the neighbourhood were beginning to get yellow for the harvest; the small patches of potatoes were under flower, and promised well; the sheep and the cattle, as if tired of feeding, had lain down to rest on the face of the hills; and the dogs, as if satisfied their services were not required for a time, chose for themselves pleasant, well-sheltered spots and lay basking at full length in the sun.

Even the little boats on the loch, though their sails were spread, made no progress, but lay at rest, reflecting their own tiny shadows on the bosom of the deep, still waters.

The scene was most enchanting; and, although old Flora's eyes were getting dim with age, she looked on the objects before her with great delight.

While the old woman was thus enjoying the benefit of the fresh air, admiring the beauty of the landscape, and just when the poor children had entered the house to prepare a frugal meal for themselves and their aged charge, a sudden barking of dogs gave signal intimation of the approach of strangers.

The native inquisitiveness of the young ones was immediately set on edge, and off they set across the fields, and over the fences, after the dogs.

They soon returned, however, with horror depicted on their countenances; they had a fearful tale to unfold.

The furniture and other effects of their nearest neighbours, just across the hill, they saw thrown out; they heard the children screaming, and they saw the factor's men putting bars and locks on the doors.

This was enough. The heart of the old woman, so recently revived and invigorated, was now set to break within her.

What was she to do? What could she do?

Absolutely nothing!

The poor children thought that if they could only get t h e i r
aged granny inside before the evicting officers arrived then all would be well.

The officers, however, arrived before they could get this accomplished; and instead of letting the old woman in, they threw out before the door every article that was inside the house, and then they placed large bars and padlocks on the door!

The grandchildren were horror-struck at this procedure — and no wonder.

Here they were, shut out of the house and home, their father and elder brother several hundred miles away from them, and their mother dead. The only shelter was a sheep cot a few hundred yards away and with some difficulty they dragged their gran there.

It was a most wretched habitation, quite unfit for human beings, yet here the widow was compelled to remain until the following December.

When her son came home from the harvest in the south, he was amazed at the treatment his aged mother and his children had received.

He was then in good health; but a few weeks in the cold and damp of the sheep cot had a most deadly effect upon his health, for he was seized with violent cramps, then with a cough; at last his limbs and body swelled, and then he died!

When dead, his corpse lay across the floor, his feet at the opposite wall, and his head being at the door, the wind waved his long black hair to and fro until he was placed in his coffin.

The inspector of the poor, who was also ground officer to Lord Macdonald, and chief officer in the evictions, at last appeared, and removed the old woman to another house; not, however, until he was threatened with prosecution for neglect of duty.

The grandchildren were also removed from the sheep cot, for they were ill; Peggy and William were seriously so, but Sandy, although ill, could walk a little.

The inspector for the poor gave the children, during their illness, only 14 lbs of meal and 3 lbs of rice, as aliment for three weeks, and nothing else.

To the grandmother he allowed two shillings and six-pence per month, but made no provision for fuel, lodgings, nutritious diet, or cordials — all of which this old woman much required.

When I visited the house where old Flora Matheson and her grandchildren reside, I found her lying on a miserable pallet of straw, which, with a few rags of clothing, are on the bare floor.

She is reduced to a skeleton, and I have no hesitation in declaring that she was then actually starving.

She had nothing whatever in the way of food but a few wet potatoes and two or three shellfish.

The picture she presented, as she lay on her wretched pallet of black rags and brown straw, with her mutch as black as soot, and her long arms thrown across, with nothing on them but the skin, was a most lamentable one — and one that reflects the deepest discredit on the parochial authorities of Strath.

There was no-one to attend to the wants or infirmities of this aged pauper but her grandchild, a young girl, ten years of age".

*   *   *   *   *   *   *   *   *

Before leaving Skye, it will be interesting to see the dif-ference of opinion which existed among the chiefs regar-ding the eviction of the people at this period and a century earlier.

We have just seen what a Lord Macdonald has done in the nineteenth century.

Let us compare his proceedings and feelings to those of his ancestor, in 1739, a century earlier

In that year a certain Norman Macleod managed to get some islanders to emigrate, and it was feared that the government would hold Sir Alexander Macdonald of Sleat responsible, as he was reported to have encouraged Macleod.

The baronet being from home, his wife, Lady Margaret, wrote to Lord Justice-Clerk Milton on the 1st of January

1740, pleading with him to use all his influence against a prosecution of her husband, which, "tho' it cannot be dangerouse to him, yett it cannot faill of being both troublesome and expensive".

She begins her letter by stating that she was informed "by different hands from Edinburgh that there is a currant report of a ship's haveing gone from thiss country with a greate many people designed for America, and that Sir Alexander is thought to have concurred in forceing these people away".

She then declares the charge against her husband to be "a falsehood", but she "is quite acquainted with the danger of a report" of that nature.

Instead of Sir Alexander being a party to the proceedings of this "Norman Macleod, with a number of fellows that he had picked up execute his intentions", he "was both angry and concern'd to hear that some of his oune people were taken in this affair".

What a contrast between the sentiments here expressed and those which carried out the modern evictions!

And yet it is well-known that, in other respects no more humane man ever lived than he who was nominally responsible for the cruelties in Skye and at Sollas.

He allowed himself to be imposed upon by others, and completely abdicated his high functions as landlord and chief of his people.

We have the most conclusive testimony and assurance from one who knew his lordship intimately, that, to his dying day, he never ceased to regret what had been done in his name, and at the time, with his tacit approval, in Skye and in North Uist.

Horror of the Quebec famine

In the summer of 1851 hundreds of islanders from BARRA and SOUTH UIST were shipped out to Canada.

The instigator of this scheme was Colonel Gordon who was proprietor of large estates on the islands.

His tenants had been promised free passage and jobs in Canada.

But there was no work when they got there and hundreds were left to starve in the freezing climate.

The following statement, made on arrival in Quebec by a group of reluctant immigrants tells a chilling story ...

'We, the undersigned, passengers per *Admiral*, from Stornoway, in the Highlands of Scotland, do solemnly depose to the following facts:— That Colonel Gordon is proprietor of estates in South Uist and Barra; that among many hundreds of tenants and cottars whom he has sent this season from his estates to Canada, he gave directions to his factor, Mr Fleming of Cluny Castle, Aberdeenshire, to ship on board of the above-named vessel a number of nearly 450 of said tenants and cottars, from the estate in Barra; that, accordingly, a great majority of these people, among whom were the undersigned, proceeded voluntarily to embark on board the *Admiral*, at Loch Boisdale, on or about the 11th August, 1851; but that several of the people who were intended to be shipped for this port, Quebec, refused to proceed on board, and, in fact, absconded from their homes to avoid the embarkation.

Whereupon Mr Fleming gave orders to a policeman, who was accompanied by the ground officer of the estate in Barra, and some constables, to pursue the people, who had run away, among the mountains; which they did, and succeeded in capturing about twenty from the mountains and islands in the neighbourhood; but only came with the officers on an attempt being made to handcuff them; and that some who ran away were not brought back, in consequence of which four families at least have been divided, some having come in the ships to Quebec, while the other members of the same families are left in the Highlands.

The undersigned further declare that those who voluntarily embarked did so under promises to the effect that Colonel Gordon would defray their passage to Quebec; that the Government Emigration Agent there would send the whole party free to Upper Canada, where, on arrival, the Government agents would give them work, and furthermore, grant them land on certain conditions.

The undersigned finally declare, that they are now landed in Quebec so destitute, that if immediate relief be not afforded them, and continued until they are settled in employment, the whole will be liable to perish from want'.

(Signed) HECTOR LAMONT
and 70 others

The Quebec Times stated in an editorial:—

"If as men the sufferings of these our fellow-creatures

find sympathy in our hearts, as Canadians their wrongs concern us more dearly.

The fifteen hundred souls whom Colonel Gordon has sent to Quebec this season have all been supported for the past week. at least, and conveyed to Upper Canada at the expense of the colony; and on their arrival in Toronto and Hamilton the greater number have been dependent on the charity of the benevolent for a morsel of bread.

Four hundred are in the river at present, and will arrive in a day or two, making a total of nearly 2000 of Colonel Gordon's tenants and cottars whom the province will have to support.

The winter is at hand, work is becoming scarce in Upper Canada. Where are these people to find food?"

The Dundas Warder paper in its issue of October 2, 1851, described the condition of the same set of people on arrival in Ontario.

"We have been pained beyond measure for some time past to witness in our streets so many unfortunate Highland emigrants, apparently destitute of any means of subsistence, and many of them sick from want and other atttendant causes.

It was pitiful the other day to view a funeral of one of these wretched people.

It was, indeed, a sad procession.

The coffin was constructed of the rudest material; a few rough boards nailed together was all that could be afforded to convey to its last resting-place the body of the homeless emigrant.

Children followed in the mournful train; perchance they followed a brother's bier, one with whom they had sported and played for many a healthful day among their native glens.

Theirs were looks of indescribable sorrow.

They were in rags; their mourning weeds were the shapeless fragments of what had once been clothes.

There was a mother, too, among the mourners, one who had tended the departed with anxious care in infancy, and had doubtless looked forward to a happier future in this land of plenty.

The anguish of her countenance told too plainly these hopes were blasted, and she was about to bury them in the grave of her child.

There will be many to sound the fulsome noise of flattery in the ear of the generous landlord, who had spent so much to assist the emigratiion of his poor tenants.

They will give him the misnomer of a *benefactor*, and for what?

Because he has rid his estates of the encumbrance of a pauper population.

Emigrants of the poorer class who arrived here from the Western Highlands of Scotland are often so situated that their emigration is more cruel than banishment.

Their last shilling is spent probably before they reach the upper province — they are reduced to the necessity of begging.

But, again, the case of those emigrants of whom we speak is rendered more deplorable from their ignorance of the English tongue.

Of the hundreds of Highlanders in and around Dundas at present, perhaps not half-a-dozen understand anything but Gaelic.

In looking at these matters, we are impressed with the conviction that, so far from emigrations being a panacea for Highland destitution, it is fraught with disasters of no ordinary magnitude to the emigrant whose previous habits, under the most favourable circumstances, render him unable to take advantage of the industry of Canada, even when brought hither free of expense.

We may assist these poor creatures for a time, but charity will scarcely bide the hungry cravings for so many in a very long period.

Mass exodus from Rum

This island, at one time, had a large population, all of whom were weeded out in the usual way.

The Rev Donald Maclean, minister of the Parish of Small Isles, informs us in *The New Statistical Account*, that "In 1826 all the inhabitants of the Island of Rum, amounting at least to 400 souls, found it necessary to leave their native land, and to seek for new abodes in the distant wilds of our colonies in America.

Of all the old residenters, only one family remained upon the Island. The old and the young, the feeble and the strong, were all united in this general emigration.

A similar emigration took place in 1828 from the Island of Muck, so that the parish has now become depopulated.

In 1831 the population of the whole parish was 1015, while before that date it was much larger.

In 1851 it was 916.

In 1881 it was reduced by 50. The total population of Rum in 1881 was 89 souls.

Hugh Miller, who visited the Island describes it and the evictions thus:—

All was solitary.

We could see among the deserted fields the grass-grown foundations of cottages razed to the ground, but the valley, more desolate than that which we had left, had not even a single inhabited dwelling; it seemed as if man had done with it for ever.

The Island, eighteen years before, had been divested of its inhabitants, amounting at the time to rather more than 400 souls, to make way for one sheep farmer and 8000 sheep.

All the aborigines of Rum crossed the Atlantic; and, at the close of 1828, the entire population consisted of but the sheep farmer, and a few shepherds, and his servants: the Island of Rum reckoned up scarce a single family at this period for every 5 square miles of area which it contained.

But depopulation on so extreme a scale was found inconvenient; the place had been rendered too thoroughly a desert for the comfort of the occupant; and on the occasion of a clearing which took place shortly after in Skye, he accommodated some 10 or 12 of the ejected families with sites for cottages, and pasturage for a few cows, on the bit of morass beside Loch Scresort, on which I had seen their humble dwellings.

But the whole of the once-peopled interior remains a wilderness, without inhabitants, — all the more lonely in its aspect from the circumstance that the solitary valleys, with their plough-furrowed patches, and their ruined heaps of stone, open up shores every whit as solitary as themselves, and that wide untrodden sea stretches drearily around.

It did not seem as if the depopulation of Rum had tended much to anyone's advantage.

Through time the single sheep farmer who had occupied the holdings of so many had been unfortunate in his speculations, and had left the Island; the proprietor, his landlord, seemed to have been as little fortunate as the tenant, for the Island itself was in the market, and a report was current at the time that it was on the eve of being purchased by some wealthy Englishman, who proposed converting it into a deer forest.

How strange a cycle! Uninhabited originally, save by wild animals, it became at an early period, a home of men, who as the grey wall on the hillside testified, derived in part at least their sustenance from the chase.

They broke in from the waste the furrowed patches on the slopes of the valleys, — they reared herds of cattle and flocks of sheep, — their number increased to nearly 500 souls, — they enjoyed the average happiness of human creatures in the present imperfect state of being, — they contributed their portion of hardy and vigorous manhood to the armies of the country, and a few of their more adventurous spirits, impatient of the narrow bounds which confined them, and a course of life little varied by incident, emigrated to America.

Then came the change of system so general in the Highlands; and the island lost all its original inhabitants, on a wool and mutton speculation, — inhabitants, the descendants of men who had chased the deer on its hills 500 years before, and who, though they recognised some wild island lord as their superior, they did him service, and regarded the place as indisputedly their own.

And now yet another change was on the eve of ensuing, and the island was to return to its original state, as a home of wild animals, where a few hunters from the mainland might enjoy the chase for a month or two every twelve months, but which could form no permanant place of human abode.

Once more a strange, and surely most melancholy cycle!

In another place the same writer asks:—

Where was the one tenant of the island, for whose sake so many others had been removed?

He then answers:—

"We found his house occupied by a humble shepherd, who had in charge the wreck of his property, — property no longer his, but held for the benefit of his creditors.

The great sheep farmer had gone down under circumstances of very general bearing, and on whose after development, when in their latent state, improving landlords had failed to calculate".

HARRIS and other Western Isles suffered in a similar manner.

Mull, Tiree, and others in Argyllshire are noticed in dealing with that county.

Poverty and misery of Argyll crofters

In many parts of Argyllshire the people have been weeded out none the less effectively, though the process generally was of a milder nature than that adopted in some of the places already described.

By some means or other, however, the ancient tenantry have largely disappeared to make room for the sheep farmer and the sportsman.

Mr Somerville, Lochgilphead, writing on this subject, says, "The watchword of all is exterminate, exterminate the native race.

Through this monomania of landlords the cottier population is all but extinct; and the substantial yeoman is undergoing the same process of dissolution". He then proceeds:—

"About 9 miles of country on the west side of Loch Awe, in Argyllshire, that formerly maintained 45 families, are now rented by one person as a sheep farm; and in the Island of Luing which formerly contained about 50 substantial farmers, besides cottiers, this number is now reduced to about six.

The work of eviction began by giving, in many cases, to the ejected population, facilities and pecuniary aid for emigration; but now the people are turned adrift, penniless and shelterless; and others, festering in our villages, form a formidable Arab population, who drink our money contributed as parochial relief".

A deputation from the Glasgow Highland Relief Board, consisting of Dr Robert Macgregor and Mr Charles R Baird, their Secretary, visited Mull, Ulva, Iona, Tiree, Coll, and part of Morvern, in 1849, and they immediately afterwards issued a printed report on the state of these places, from which a few extracts will prove instructive.

They inform us that the population of the Island of Mull according to the Government Census of 1821, was 10,612; in 1841, 10,064.

In 1871, we find it reduced to 6,441, and by the Census of 1881, now before us, it is stated at 5,624, or a fraction more than half the number that inhabited the Island in 1821.

TOBERMORY, we are told, "has been for some time the resort of the greater part of the small crofters and cottars, *ejected* from their holdings and houses on the surrounding estates, and thus there has been a great accumulation of distress".

Then we are told that "severe as the destitution has been in the rural districts, we think it has been still more so in Tobermory and other villages" — a telling comment on, and reply to, those who would now have us believe that the evictors of those days and of our own were acting the character of wise benefactors when they ejected the people from the inland and rural districts of the various counties to wretched villages, and rocky hamlets on the sea-shore.

ULVA. — The population of the Island of Ulva in 1849 was 360 souls.

The reporters state that a "large portion" of it "has lately been converted into a sheep farm, and consequently a number of small crofters and cottars have been warned away" by Mr Clark.

"Some of these will find great difficulty in settling themselves anywhere, and all of them have little prospect of employment ... Whatever may be the ultimate effect to the landowners of the conversion of a number of small crofts into large farms, we need scarcely say that this process is causing much poverty and misery among the crofters".

How Mr Clark carried out his intention of evicting the tenantry of Ulva may be seen from the fact that the population of 360 souls, in 1849 was reduced to 51 in 1881.

KILFINICHEN. — In this district we are told that "The crofters and cottars having been warned off, 26 individuals emigrated to America, at their own expense, and one at that of the Parochial Board; a good many removed to Kinloch, where they are now in great poverty, and those who remained were not allowed to cultivate any ground for crop or even garden stuffs.

The stock and other effects of a number of crofters on Kinloch last year (1848), whose rents averaged from £5 to £15 per annum, having been sequestrated and sold, these parties are now reduced to a state of pauperism, having no employment or means of subsistence whatever".

As to the cottars, it is said that "the great mass of them are now in a very deplorable state".

On the estate of GRIBUN, Colonel Macdonald of Inchkenneth, the proprietor, gave the people plenty of work, by which they were quite independent of relief from any quarter, and the character which he gives to the deputation of the people generally is most refreshing, when we compare it with the baseless charges usually made against them by the majority of his class.

The reporters state that "Colonel Macdonald spoke in high terms of the honesty of the people and of their great patience and forbearance under their severe privations".

It is gratifying to be able to record this simple act of justice, not only as the people's due, but specially to the credit of Colonel Macdonald's memory and goodness of heart.

BUNESSAN. — Respecting this district, belonging to the Duke of Argyll, our authority says:— "It will be recollected that the (Relief) Committee, some time ago, advanced £128 to assist in procuring provisions for a number of emigrants from the Duke of Argyll's estate, in the Ross of Mull and Iona, in all 243 persons — 125 adults and 118 children.

When there, we made inquiry into the matter, and were informed (by those, as it proved, quite ignorant of the facts) that the emigration had been productive of much good, as the parties who emigrated could not find the means of subsistence in this country, and had every *prospect* of doing so in Canada, where all of them had relations; and also because the land occupied by some of these emigrants had been given to increase the crofts of others.

Since our return home, however, we have received the very melancholy and distressing intelligence, that many of these emigrants had been seized with cholera on their arrival in Canada; that not a few of them had fallen victims to it; and that the survivors had suffered great privations".

Compare the "prospect" of much good, predicted for these poor creatures, with the sad reality of having been forced away to die a terrible death immediately on their arrival on a foreign shore!

IONA, at this time, contained a population of 500, reduced in 1881 to 243. It also is the property of the Duke of Argyll, as well as

The ISLAND OF TIREE, the population of which is given in the report as follows:— In 1755, it was 1509, increasing in 1777, to 1681; in 1801, to 2416; in 1821, to 4181; and in 1841 to 4687.

In 1849 "after considerable emigrations", it was 3903; while in 1881, it was reduced to 2733.

The deputation recommended emigration from Tiree as imperatively necessary, but they "call especial attention to the necessity of emigration being conducted on proper principles, or, 'on a system calculated to promote the permanent benefit of those who emigrate, and of those who remain', because we have reason to fear that not a few parties in these districts are anxious to get rid of the small crofters and cottars at all hazard, and without making sufficient provision for their future comfort and settlement elsewhere; and because we have seen the very distressing account of the privations and sufferings of the poor people who emigrated from Tiree and the Ross of Mull to Canada this year (1849), and would spare no pains to prevent a recurrence of such deplorable circumstances.

As we were informed that the Duke of Argyll had expended nearly £1200 on account of the emigrants (in all 247 souls) from Tiree; as the Committee advanced £131.15s. to purchase provisions for them; and as funds were remitted to Montreal to carry them up the country, we sincerely trust that the account we have seen of their sufferings in Canada is somewhat over-charged, and that it is not at all events to be ascribed to want of due provision being made for them, ere they left this country, to carry them to their destination.

Be this as it may, however, we trust that no emigration will in future be promoted by proprietors or others, which will not secure, as far as human efffort can, *the benefit of those who emigrate,* as well as of those who are left at home ...

Being aware of the poverty of the great majority of the inhabitants of this island, and of the many difficulties with which they have to contend, we were agreeably surprised to find their dwellings remarkably neat and clean — very superior indeed, both externally and internally, to those of the other islands; nay, more, such as would bear comparison with cottages in any part of the kingdom.

The inhabitants, too, we believe, are active and enterprising, and, if once put in a fair way of doing so, would soon raise themselves to comfort and independence".

Very good, indeed, Tiree!

THE ISLAND OF COLL, which is separated from Tiree by a channel only two miles in width, had a population, in 1755, of 1193; in 1771, of 1200; in 1801, of 1162; in 1821, of 1264. In 1841 it reached 1409.

At the time of the visit from the deputation, from whose

report we quote, the population of the Island was down to 1235; while in 1881 it had fallen to 643.

The deputation report that during the destitution the work done by the Coll people "approximates, if it does exceed, the supplies given"; they are "hard working and industrious ... We saw considerable tracts of ground which we were assured might be reclaimed and cultivated with profit, and are satisfied that fishing is a resource capable of great improvement, and at which, therefore, many of the people might be employed to advantage; we are disposed to think that, by a little attention and prudent outlay of capital, the condition of the people here might ere long be greatly improved.

The grand difficulty in the way, however, is want of capital.

Mr Maclean, the principal proprietor, always acted most liberally when he had it in his power to do so, but, unfortunately, he has no longer the ability, and the other two proprietors are also under trust".

Notwithstanding these possibilities the population is undergoing a constant process of diminution.

We shall now return to the mainland portion of the county and the parish of Ardnamurchan (through statements of eye-witnesses and an 1892 Deer Forest Commission report).

("Uaine gu'm mullach" (green to their tops!)

So Dr Norman Macleod described the bens of Ardnamurchan in his inimitable sketch, the "Emigrant Ship", and so they appear even to this day.

Their beautiful slopes show scarcely a vestige of heather, but an abundance of rich, sweet grass of a quality eminently suitable for pasturage.

As the steamboat passenger sails northward through the Sound of Mull, he sees straight ahead, and stretching at right angles across his course, a long range of low hills culminating in a finely-shaped mass which seems to rise abruptly from the edge of the sea.

The hills are those of Ardnamurchan, and the dominating pile is Ben Hiant, 1729 feet in height, and "green to its top".

Around the base of the mountain and for miles in every direction the land is fair, fertile, and well adapted either for arable or grazing purposes.

Down to the second decade of the eighteenth century it supported about twenty-six families, which were distributed over the component townships of Coire-mhuilinn, Skinid, Buarblaig, and Tornamona.

At one sweep, the whole place was cleared, and the grounds added to the adjacent sheep farm of Mingary.

The evictions were carried out in 1828, the process being attended with many acts of heartless cruelty on the part of the laird's representatives.

In one case a half-witted woman who flatly refused to flit, was locked up in her cottage, the door being barricaded on the outside by mason-work.

She was visited every morning to see if she had arrived at a tractable frame of mind, but for days she held out.

It was not until her slender store of food was exhausted that she ceased to argue with the inevitable and decided to capitulate.

It is to cases of this character that Dr John MacLachlan, the Sweet Singer of Rahoy, referred in the lines —
"An dall, an seann duine san oinid
Toirt am mallachd air do bhuaireas".
(The blind, the aged, and the imbecile calling curses on thy greed).

The proprietor at whose instance these "removals" were carried out was Sir James Milles Riddell, Bart.

Of the dislodged families a few were given small patches of waste land, some were given holdings in various townships on the estate — the crofts of which were subdivided for their accommodation — and some were forced to seek sanctuary beyond the Atlantic.

Additional clearances were affected on the Ardnamurchan estate in 1853, when Swordle-chaol, Swordle-mhor, and Swordle-chorrach, with an aggregate area of about 3000 acres, were divested of their crofting population, and thrown into a single sheep farm.

Swordle-chaol was occupied by four tenants, Swordle-mhor by six, and Swordle-chorrach by six.

Five years previous to the evictions, all the crofters came under a written obligation to the proprietor to build new dwelling-houses.

The walls were to be of stone and lime, 40 ft long, 17½ ft wide, and 7½ ft high.

The houses, two-gabled, were to have each two rooms and a kitchen, with wooden ceiling and floors, the kitchen alone to be floored with flags.

By the end of 1851 all the tenants had faithfully implemented their promise, and the work of building was quite completed.

Tradesmen had been employed in every case, and the cost averaged from £45 to £50.

When the people were ejected, two years later, they received no compensation whatever for their labours and outlays.

They were not even permitted to remove a door, a window, or a fixed cupboard.

The Swordle tenants were among the best-to-do on the estate, and not one of them owed the proprietor a shilling in the way of arrears of rent.

When cast adrift, the majority of them were assigned "holdings" of one acre or so in the rough lands of Sanna and Portuairk, where they had to start to reclaim peatbogs and to build for themselves housings and steadings.

Sir James Milles Riddell was the proprietor responsible for clearing the Swordles as well as the Ben Hiant townships.

Other places which he divested of people and placed under sheep were Laga, held by eight tenants, and Tarbert, which was in the hands of four.

The population of Morven parish in 1755 was 1223; in 1795 it increased to 1764; in 1801 to 2000; in 1821, it was 1995; in 1831, it rose to 2137; and in 1841 it came down to 1781; in 1871, it was only 973; while in the Census Returns for 1881 we find it stated at 741, or less than one-third of what it was fifty years before.

The late Dr Norman Macleod, after describing the happy state of things which existed in this parish before the clearances, wrote in 'Reminiscences of a Highland Parish':

"But all this was changed when those tacksmen were swept away to make room for the large sheep farms, and when the remnants of the people flocked from their empty glens to occupy houses in wretched villages near the seashore, by way of becoming fishers — often where no fish could be caught.

The result has been that 'the Parish', for example, which once had a population of 2200 souls, and received only £11 per annum from public (Church) funds for the support of the poor, expends now (1863) under the poor law upwards of £600 annually, with a population diminished by one-half (since diminished to one-third) and with poverty increased in a greater ratio ..."

GLENORCHY, of which the Marquis of Breadalbane is sole proprietor, was, like many other places, ruthlessly cleared of its whole native population.

The writer of the New Statistical Account of the Parish, in 1843, the Rev Duncan Maclean, "Fior Ghael" of the *Teachdaire,* informs us that the census taken by Dr Webster in 1755, and by Dr MacIntyre forty years later, in 1795, "differ exceedingly little", only to the number of sixty.

The Marquis of the day, it is well known, was a good friend of his reverence; the feeling was naturally reciprocated, and one of the apparent results is that the reverend author abstained from giving, in his Account of the Parish, the population statistics of the Glenorchy district.

It was, however, impossible to pass over that important part of his duty altogether, and, apparently with reluctance, he makes the following sad admission:—

"A great and rapid decrease has, however, taken place since (referring to the population in 1795).

This decrease is mainly attributable to the introduction of sheep, and the absorption of small into large tenements.

The aboriginal population of the parish of Glenorchy (not of Inishail) has been nearly supplanted by adventurers from the neighbouring district of Breadalbane, who now occupy the far largest share of the parish.

There are a few, and only a few, shoots from stems that supplied the ancient population.

Some clans, who were rather numerous and powerful, have disappeared altogether; others, viz., the Downies, Macnabs, Macnicols, and Fletchers, have nearly ceased to exist.

The Macgregors, at one time lords of the soil, have totally disappeared; not one of the name is to be found among the population.

The Macintyres, at once time extremely numerous, are likewise greatly reduced".

By this nobleman's mania for evictions, the population of Glenorchy was reduced from 1806 in 1831 to 831 in 1841, or by nearly a thousand souls in the short space of ten years!

It is, however, gratifying to find that it has since, under wise management, very largely increased.

In spite of all this we have been seriously told that there has been no depopulation of the county in the rural districts.

In this connection, some very extraordinary public utterances were recently made by two gentlemen closely connected with the county of Argyll, questioning or attempting to explain away statements, made in the House of Commons by Mr D H Macfarlane, MP, to the effect that the rural population was, from various causes, fast disappearing from the Highlands.

These utterances were — one by a no less distinguished person than the Duke of Argyll, who published his remarkable propositions in the *Times*; the other by Mr John Ramsay, MP, the Islay distiller, who imposed his baseless statement on his brother members in the House of Commons.

These oracles should have known better.

They must clearly have taken no trouble whatever to ascertain the facts for themselves, or, having ascertained them, kept them back that the public might be misled on a question with which, it is obvious to all, the personal interests of both are largely mixed up.

Let us see how the assertions of these authorities agreed with the actual facts. In 1831 the population of the county of Argyll was 100,973; in 1841 it was 97,371; in 1851 it was reduced to 88,567; and in 1881 it was down to 76,468.

Of the latter number the Registrar-General classifies 30,387 as urban, or the population of "towns and villages", leaving us only 46,081 as the total rural population of the county of Argyll at the date of the last Census, in 1881.

In 1911 the total population for the county had dropped to 70,902.

It will be necessary to keep in mind that in 1831 the county could not be said to have had many "town and village" inhabitants — not more than from 12,000 to 15,000 at most.

These resided chiefly in Campbeltown, Inveraray, and Oban; and if we deduct from the total population for that year, numbering 100,973, even the larger estimate, 15,000 of an urban or town population, we have still left, in 1831, an actual rural population of 85,973, or within a fraction of double the whole rural population of the county in 1881.

In other words, the rural population of Argyllshire was reduced in fifty years from 85,973 to 46,081, or nearly by one-half.

Canadian acres for Arran families — a Duke's pledge

In 1828 Alexander, tenth Duke of Hamilton, decided that he would make large farms on his estate and the land rented by twenty-seven families was converted into one large farm.

For various reasons, the islanders had for many years been discontented, and there seemed no hope of a change for the better.

If a man worked his place in a progressive way and made improvements on the farm, the benefit accrued solely to the landed proprietor, who thanked the good tenant by promptly raising his rent.

If the farmer objected to paying more rent, his only alternative was to submit to be turned off his holding at the expiration of his lease; then the landlord would collect the increased rent from the new tenant.

So when the duke made overtures to a large number of his tenants to the effect that if they would make room for him by getting away from their ancestral moorings in Arran, he would see that they were well provided for in the new world, it is not to be wondered at that they accepted his proposition.

It is so nice when you are cast out to be told where you can go, and be directed what to do.

The Duke promised to secure for each family a grant of 100 acres of land in Canada, and the same amount of land for each son in the family who at that time had reached the age of 21.

Arrived at their destination at Johnston Ford, province of Quebec, each family constructed a tent by stretching blankets, quilts, etc., over poles suitably disposed and tied together at the top with withes and ropes.

Fortunately the season was favourable and fires were needed only for cooking.

As just stated, the Duke of Hamilton had promised that each family and each young man who had attained his majority should receive a grant of 100 acres of land; but, when the colony was actually on the scene, the Government officials refused to give a grant except to the heads of families.

The matter of grants has been so variously stated that it is difficult to determine what the conditions were, but it appears that the actual agreement of the Duke of Hamilton was that grants should be given for two years only.

Those who came out in 1829 and 1830 secured certain grants after a delay. Those, however, who did not arrive till 1831 were told by the agents that grants were no longer to be had.

The high price they paid in Perthshire

In 1851 the population of the district known as the quod sacra parish of Rannoch numbered altogether 1800; at the census of 1881 it was below 900.

Even in 1851 it was not nearly what it was earlier.

Why this constant decrease? Several no doubt left the district voluntarily; but the great bulk of those who left were evicted.

Take, first, the Slios Min, north side of Loch Rannoch.

Fifty years ago the farm of Ardlarich, near the west end, was tenanted by three farmers, who were in good circumstances.

These were turned out to make room for one large farmer, who was rouped out last year, penniless; and the farm is now tenantless.

The next place, further east is the township of Killichoan, containing about 30 to 40 houses, with small crofts attached to each.

The crofters here are very comfortable and happy, and their houses and crofts are models of what industry, thrift and good taste can effect.

Further east is the farm of Liaran, now tenantless.

Fifty years ago it was farmed by several tenants who were turned out to make room for one man, and that at a lower rent than was paid by the former tenants.

Further, in the same direction, there are Aulich, Craganour, and Annat, every one of them tenantless.

These three farms, lately in the occupation of one tenant, and for which he paid a rental of £900, at one time maintained fifty to sixty families in comfort, all of whom have vanished, or were virtually banished from their native land.

It is only right to say that the present proprietor is not responsible for the evictions of any of the smaller tenants; the deed was done before he came into possession.

On the contrary, he is very kind to his crofter tenantry, but unfortunately for him he inherits the fruits of bad policy which has been the ruin of the Rannoch estates.

Then take the Slios Garbh, south side of Loch Rannoch.

Beginning in the west end, we have Georgetown, which, about fifty years ago, contained 25 or 26 houses, every one of which was knocked down by the late laird of Struan , and the people evicted.

The crofters of Finnart were ejected in the same way.

Next comes the township of Camghouran; a place pretty similar to Killichoan, but smaller.

The people are very industrious, cleanly, and fairly comfortable, reflecting much credit upon themselves and the present proprietor.

Next comes Dall, where there used to be a number of tenants, but now in the hands of the proprietor, an Englishman.

The estate of Innerhaden comes next. It used to be divided into ten lots — two held by the laird, and eight by as many tenants.

The whole is now in the hands of one family.

The rest of Bun-Rannoch includes the estates of Dalchosnie, Lassintullich, and Crossmount, where there used to be a large number of small tenants — most of them well-to-do but now held by five.

Lastly, take the north side of the River Dubhag, which flows out from Loch Rannoch, and is erroneously called the Tummel.

Kinloch, Druimchurn, and Druimchaisteil, always in the hands of three tenants, are now held by one.

Drumaglass contains a small number of holdings, with good houses on many of them.

Balmore, which always had six tenants in it, has now only one, the remaining portion of it being laid out in grass parks.

Ballintuim, with a good house upon it, is tenantless.

Auchitarsin, where there used to be twenty houses, is now reduced to four.

The author of the *New Statistical Account*, writing of the parish of Fortingall, of which the district referred to by our correspondent forms a part, says:—

"At present (1838) no part of the parish is more populous than it was in 1790; whereas in several districts, the population has since decreased one-half; and the same will be found to have taken place, though not perhaps in so great a proportion, in most or all of the pastoral districts of the county".

According to the census of 1801, the population was 3875; in 1811, 3236; in 1821, 3189; in 1831, 3067; and in 1881, it was reduced to 1690.

Upwards of 120 families, the same writer says, "crossed the Atlantic from this parish, since the previous Account was drawn up (in 1791), besides many individuals of both sexes; while many others have sought a livelihood in the Low Country, especially in the great towns of Edinburgh, Glasgow, Dundee, Perth, Crieff, and others.

The system of uniting several farms together, and letting them to one individual, has, more than any other circumstance produced this result".

*　　*　　*　　*　　*　　*　　*　　*　　*

Mr R Alister, author of *Barriers to the National Prosperity of Scotland*, had a controversy with the Marquis of BREADALBANE in 1853, about the eviction of his tenantry.

In a letter, dated July of that year Mr Alister made a charge against his lordship, which, for obvious reasons, he never attempted to answer, as follows:—

"Your lordship states that in reality there has been no depopulation of the district.

This, and other parts of your lordship's letter, would certainly lead any who know nothing of the facts to suppose that there had been no clearings on the Breadalbane estates; whereas it is generally believed that your lordship removed, since 1834, no less than five hundred families!

Some may think this is a small matter; but I do not.

I think it is a great calamity for a family to be thrown out, destitute of the means of life, without a roof over their heads, and cast upon the wide sea of an unfeeling world.

In Glenqueich, near Amulree, some sixty families formerly lived, where there are now only four or five; and in America, there is a glen inhabited now by its ousted tenants, called Glenqueich still.

Yet forsooth, it is maintained that there has been no depopulation here!

The desolations here look like the ruins of Irish cabins, although the population of Glenqueich were always characterised as being remarkably thrifty, economical, and wealthy.

On the Braes of Taymouth, at the back of Drummond Hill, and at Tullochyoule, some forty or fifty families formerly resided, where there is not one now.

Glenorchy, by the returns of 1831, showed a population of 1806; in 1841, 831; — there is no depopulation there?

Is it true that in Glenetive there were sixteen tenants a year or two ago, where there is not a single one now?

Is it true, my lord, that you purchased an island on the west coast called Luing, where some twenty-five families lived at the beginning of *this year,* but who are now cleared off to make room for one tenant, for whom an extensive steading is now being erected?

If my information be correct, I shall allow the public to draw their own conclusions; but, from everything that I have heard, I believe your lordship has done more to exterminate the Scottish peasantry than any man now living; and perhaps you ought to be ranked next to the Marquis of Stafford in the clearing celebrities.

If I have over-estimated the clearances at five hundred families, please correct me".

As we have already said, his lordship thought it prudent, and by far the best policy, not to make the attempt.

It is, however, gratifying to know that the present lord of Breadalbane, who is descended from a different and remote branch of the family, is an excellent landlord, and takes an entirely different view of his duties and relationship to the tenants on his vast property.

'Incredible' journeys of ten thousand — by Sheriff

Mr Robert Brown, Sheriff-Substitute of the Western District of Inverness-shire, in summing up the number who left from 1801 to 1803, says:—

"In the year 1801, a Mr George Dennon, from Pictou, carried out two cargoes of emigrants from Fort William to Pictou, consisting of about seven hundred souls.

A vessel sailed the same season from Isle Martin with about one hundred passengers, it is believed, from the same place.

No more vessels sailed that year; but in 1802, eleven large ships sailed with emigrants to America.

Of these, four were from Fort William, one from Knoydart, one from Isle Martin, one from Uist, one from Greenock.

Five of these were bound for Canada, four for Pictou, and one for Cape Breton.

The only remaining vessel, which took a cargo of people in Skye, sailed for Wilmington, in the United States.

In the year 1803, exclusive of Lord Selkirk's transport, eleven cargoes of emigrants went from the North Highlands.

Of these, four were from the Moray Firth, two from Ullapool, three from Stornoway, and two from Fort William.

The whole of these cargoes were bound for the British settlements, and most of them were discharged at Pictou".

Soon after, several other vessels sailed from the North West Highlands with emigrants, the whole of whom were for the British Colonies.

In addition to these, Lord Selkirk took out 250 from South Uist in 1802, and in 1803 he sent out to Prince Edward Island about 800 souls, in three different vessels, most of whom were from the Island of Skye, and the remainder from Ross-shire, North Argyll, the interior of the county of Inverness, and the Island of Uist.

In 1804, 1805, and 1806, several cargoes of Highlanders left Mull, Skye, and Western Islands, for Prince Edward Island and other North American Colonies.

Altogether, not less than 10,000 souls left the Western Highlands and Islands during the first six years of the present century, a fact which will now appear incredible.

*   *   *   *   *   *   *   *   *

Sir Walter Scott wrote:—

"In too many instances the Highlands have been drained, not of their superfluity of population, but the whole mass of the inhabitants, dispossessed by an unrelenting avarice, which will be one day found to have been as short-sighted as it is unjust and selfish.

Meantime, the Highlands may become the fairy ground for romance and poetry, or the subject of experiment for the professors of speculation, political and economical.

But if the hour of need should come, and it may not, perhaps, be far distant — the pibroch may sound through the deserted region but the summons will remain unanswered."

Voyage of despair
for pilgrim band

The reader is already acquainted with the misery endured by those evicted from Barra and South Uist by Colonel Gordon, after their arrival in Canada.

This was no isolated case.

We shall here give a few instances of the unspeakable suffering of those pioneers who left so early as 1773, in the ship *Hector*, for Pictou, Nova Scotia.

The *Hector* was owned by two men, Pagan and Witherspoon who bought three shares of land in Pictou, and they engaged a Mr John Ross as their agent, to accompany the vessel to Scotland, to bring out as many colonists as could be induced, by misrepresentation and falsehoods, to leave their homes.

They offered a free passage, a farm, and a year's free provisions to their dupes.

On his arrival in Scotland, Ross drew a glowing picture of the land and other manifold advantages of the country to which he was enticing the people.

The Highlanders knew nothing of the difficulties awaiting them in a land covered over with a dense unbroken forest.

Calling first at Greenock, three families and five single young men joined the vessel at that port.

She then sailed to Lochbroom in Ross-shire, where she received 33 families and 25 single men, the whole of her passengers numbering about 200 souls.

This band, in the beginning of July, 1773, bade a final farewell to their native land, not a soul on board having ever crossed the Atlantic except a single sailor and John Ross, the agent.

As they were leaving, a piper came on board who had not paid his passage; the captain ordered him ashore, but the strains of the national instrument affected those on board so much that they pleaded to have him allowed to accompany them, and offered to share their own rations with him in exchange for his music during the passage.

Their request was granted, and his performance aided

in no small degree to cheer the noble band of pioneers in their long voyage of eleven weeks, in a miserable hulk, across the Atlantic.

The pilgrim band kept up their spirits as best they could by song, pipe music, dancing, wrestling, and other amusements, through the long and painful voyage.

The ship was so rotten that the passengers could pick the wood out of her sides with their fingers.

They met with a severe gale off the Newfoundland coast, and were driven back by it so far that it took them about fourteen days to get back to the point at which the storm met them.

The accommodation was wretched, smallpox and dysentery broke out among the passengers.

Eighteen of the children died, and were committed to the deep amidst such anguish and heart-rending agony as only a Highlander can understand.

Their stock of provisions became almost exhausted, the water became scarce and bad; the remnants of provision left consisted mainly of salt meat, which, from the scarcity of water, added greatly to their sufferings.

The oatcake carried by them became mouldy, so that much of it had been thrown away before they dreamt of having such a long passage.

Fortunately for them, one of the passengers, Hugh Macleod, more prudent than the others, gathered up the despised scraps into a bag, and during the last few days of the voyage his fellows were too glad to join him in devouring this refuse to keep souls and bodies together.

At last the *Hector* dropped anchor in the harbour, opposite where the town of Pictou now stands.

Though the Highland dress was then proscribed at home, this emigrant band carried theirs along with them, and, in celebration of their arrival, many of the younger men donned their national dress — to which a few of them were able to add the *Sgian Dubh* and the Claymore — while the piper blew up his pipes with might and main, its thrilling tones, for the first time, startling the denizens of the endless forest, and its echoes resounding through the wild solitude.

Scottish emigrants are admitted upon all hands to have given its backbone of moral and religious strength to the Province, and to those brought over from the Highlands in this vessel is due the honour of being in the forefront — the pioneers and vanguard.

But how different was the reality to the expectations of these poor creatures, led by the plausibility of the emigration agent, to expect free estates on their arrival.

The whole scene, as far as the eye could see, was a dense forest.

They crowded on the deck to take stock of their future home, and their hearts sank within them.

They were landed without the provisions promised, without shelter of any kind, and were only able, by the aid of those few before them, to erect camps of the rudest and most primitive description, to shelter their wives and their children from the elements.

Their feelings of disappointment were most bitter.

Many of them sat down in the forest and wept bitterly; hardly any provisions were possessed leaving them almost destitute.

It was now too late to raise any crops that year.

To make matters worse, they were sent some three miles into the forest, so that they could not even take advantage with the same ease of any fish that might be caught in the harbour.

The whole thing appeared an utter mockery.

To unskilled men the work of clearing seemed hopeless; they were naturally afraid of the Red Indian and of the wild beasts of the forest; without roads or paths, they were frightened to move for fear of getting lost.

It would be tedious to describe the sufferings which they afterwards endured. Many of them left.

Others, fathers, mothers, and children, bound themselves away, as virtual slaves, in other settlements, for mere subsistence.

Those who remained lived in small huts, covered only with the bark of branches of trees to shelter them from the bitter winter cold.

They had to walk some eighty miles, through a trackless forest, in deep snow to Truro, to obtain a few bushels of potatoes, or a little flour in exchange for their labour, dragging these back all the way again on their backs, and endless cases of great suffering from actual want occurred.

In the following spring they set to work. They cleared some of the forest, and planted a larger crop.

They learned to hunt the moose, a kind of large deer.

They began to cut timber, and sent a cargo of it from Pictou — the first of a trade very profitably and extensively carried on ever since.

The population had, however, grown less than it was before their arrival; for in this year it amounted to only 78 persons.

One of the modes of laying up a supply of food for the winter was to dig up a large quantity of clams or large oysters, pile them in large heaps on the sea-shore, and then cover them over with sand, though they were often, in winter, obliged to cut through ice more than a foot thick to get to them.

This will give a fair idea of the hardships experienced by the earlier emigrants in these colonies.

In Prince Edward Island, however, a colony from Lockerbie, in Dumfriesshire, who came out in 1774, seemed to have fared even worse.

They began operations on the Island with fair prospects of success, when a plague of locusts, or field mice, broke out, and consumed everything, even the potatoes in the ground; and for eighteen months the settlers experienced all the miseries of a famine, having for several months only what lobsters or shell-fish they could gather from the sea-shore.

The winter brought them to such a state of weakness that they were unable to convey food a reasonable distance even when they had means to buy it.

Who can think of these early hardships and cruel existences without condemning — even hating — the memories of the harsh and heartless Highland and Scottish lairds, who made existence at home even almost as miserable for those noble fellows, and who then drove them in thousands out of their native land, not caring one iota whether they sank in the Atlantic, or were starved to death on a strange and uncongenial soil?

Retributive justice demands that posterity should execrate the memories of the authors of such misery and horrid cruelty.

It may seem uncharitable to write thus of the dead; but it is impossible to forget their inhuman conduct, though, no thanks to them, it has turned out for the better, for the descendants of those who were banished to what was then infinitely worse than transportation for the worst crimes. Such criminals were looked after and cared for; but those poor fellows, driven out of their homes by the Highland lairds, and sent across there, were left to starve, helpless, and uncared for.